CONTENTS:

FIXING MISTAKES

500 most-commonly misspelled words ------------------- 01
Homophones and their meanings -------------------------- 05
Easily-confused words and meanings --------------------- 17

LITERACY / KNOWLEDGE

Terms to know by grade – index of terms ---------------- 25
Terms to know through grade 8 -------------------------- 31
Terms to know through grade 9 -------------------------- 39
Terms to know through grade 10 ------------------------- 46
Terms to know through grade 11 ------------------------- 55
Terms to know through grade 12 ------------------------- 60

USAGE / GRAMMAR

Capitalization -- 61
Italics -- 63
Quotation Marks -- 64
Numbers -- 65
Semi-colon --- 66
Colon --- 67
Apostrophe --- 68
Dash and Parenthesis ------------------------------------- 69
Quotation Marks / Long Quotations ------------------- 70
Comma --- 72

WRITING AND RESEARCHING WELL

Transitional words and phrases ----------------------------------- 74
The writing process --- 77
Key words in writing assignments & exams --------------- 78
Evaluating sources --- 80
Formatting manuscripts --- 85
Title pages -- 86

CITATION AND SOURCING

MLA Citation
    Introduction to the format ----------------------------- 89
    In-Text citation -- 90
    Works-cited page --- 101

Chicago-style Citation
    Introduction to the format ----------------------------- 119
    Footnoting and Bibliography ---------------------- 122

NOTES

Personal notes --- 141

500 MOST-COMMONLY MISSPELLED WORDS

absence
abundance
accessible
accidentally
acclaim
accommodate
accomplish
accordion
accumulate
achievement
acquaintance
acquire
acquitted
across
address
advertisement
advice
advise
affect
alleged
amateur
analysis
analyze
annual
apartment
apparatus
apparent
appearance
arctic
argument
ascend
atheist
athletic
attendance
auxiliary

balloon
barbecue
bargain
basically
beggar

beginning
belief
believe
beneficial
benefit
biscuit
boundaries
business

calendar
camouflage
candidate
category
cemetery
challenge
changeable
changing
characteristic
chief
climbed
clothes
clothing
cloth
collectible
colonel
column
coming
commission
committee
commitment
comparative
competent
completely
concede
conceivable
conceive
condemn
condescend
conscience
conscientious
conscious

consistent
continuous
controlled
controversial
controversy
convenient
correlate
correspondence
counselor
courteous
courtesy
criticize
criticism

deceive
defendant
deferred
definitely
definition
dependent
descend
describe
description
desirable
despair
desperate
develop
dictionary
difference
dilemma
dining
disappearance
disappoint
disastrous
discipline
disease
dispensable
dissatisfied
dominant

1

easily	forfeit	independence
ecstasy	formerly	independent
effect	foresee	indicted
efficiency	forty	indispensable
eighth	fourth	inevitable
either	fuelling	influential
eligible	fulfill	information
eliminate	fundamentally	inoculate
embarrass		insurance
emperor	gauge	intelligence
encouragement	generally	interference
enemy	genius	interrupt
encouraging	government	introduce
entirely	governor	irrelevant
environment	grammar	irresistible
equipped	grievous	island
equivalent	guarantee	
especially	guardian	jealousy
exaggerate	guerrilla	judicial
exceed	guidance	knowledge
excellence		laboratory
exhaust	handkerchief	laid
existence	happily	later
existent	harass	latter
expense	height	legitimate
experience	heinous	leisure
experiment	hemorrhage	length
explanation	heroes	license
extremely	hesitancy	lieutenant
exuberance	hindrance	lightning
	hoarse	likelihood
facsimile	hoping	likely
fallacious	humorous	loneliness
fallacy	hygiene	loose
familiar	hypocrisy	lose
fascinating	hypocrite	losing
feasible		lovely
February	ideally	luxury
fictitious	idiosyncrasy	
fiery	ignorance	magazine
finally	imaginary	maintain
financially	immediately	maintenance
fluorescent	implement	manageable
forcibly	incidentally	maneuver
foreign	incredible	manufacture

2

mathematics	optimism	precedence
medicine	optimistic	preceding
millennium	orchestra	preference
millionaire	ordinarily	preferred
miniature	origin	prejudice
minuscule	outrageous	preparation
minutes	overrun	prescription
miscellaneous		prevalent
mischievous	pamphlets	primitive
missile	parallel	principal
misspelled	particular	principle
mortgage	pavilion	privilege
mosquito	peaceable	probably
mosquitoes	peculiar	procedure
murmur	penetrate	proceed
muscle	perceive	profession
mysterious	performance	professor
	permanent	prominent
narrative	permissible	pronounce
naturally	permissible	pronunciation
nauseous	permitted	propaganda
necessary	perseverance	psychology
necessity	persistence	publicly
neighbor	personal	pursue
neutron	personnel	
ninety	perspiration	quantity
noticeable	physical	quarantine
nowadays	physician	questionnaire
nuisance	piece	quizzes
	pilgrimage	
obedience	pitiful	realistically
obstacle	planning	realize
occasion	pleasant	really
occasionally	portray	recede
occurred	possess	receipt
occurrence	possession	receive
official	possessive	recognize
omission	potato	recommend
omit	potatoes	reference
omitted	possibility	referring
opinion	possible	relevant
opponent	practically	relieving
opportunity	prairie	religious
oppression	precede	remembrance

3

reminiscence	sponsor	twelfth
repetition	spontaneous	tyranny
representative	statistics	
resemblance	stopped	unanimous
reservoir	strategy	undoubtedly
resistance	strength	unforgettable
restaurant	strenuous	unique
rheumatism	stubbornness	unnecessary
rhythm	studying	usable
rhyme	subordinate	usage
rhythmical	subtle	usually
ridiculous	succeed	utilization
	success	
sacrilegious	succession	vacuum
sacrifice	sufficient	valuable
safety	supersede	vengeance
salary	suppress	vigilant
satellite	surprise	village
scary	surround	villain
scenery	susceptible	violence
schedule	suspicious	visible
secede	syllable	vision
secretary	symmetrical	virtue
seize	synonymous	volume
sense		
sentence	tangible	warrant
separate	technical	warriors
separation	technique	weather
sergeant	temperamental	Wednesday
several	temperature	weird
severely	tendency	wherever
shepherd	themselves	whether
shining	theories	which
siege	therefore	wholly
similar	thorough	willful
simile	though	Willfully
simply	through	withdrawal
simultaneous	tomorrow	woman
sincerely	tournament	women
skiing	towards	worthwhile
sophomore	tragedy	writing
souvenir	transferring	
specifically	tries	yacht
specimen	truly	yield
		young

4

HOMOPHONES AND ~~THERE~~ THEIR MEANINGS

Homophones are two or more words that have the same pronunciation, but (usually) different spelling, meaning, and origin. Using the right one is important.

acts (deeds)
ax (tool)

ad (advertisement)
add (addition)

ads (advertisements)
adz (ax-like tool)

aid (assistance)
aide (a helper)

ail (be sick)
ale (beverage)

air (oxygen)
heir (successor)

aisle (path)
I'll (I will)
isle (island)

all (everything)
awl (tool)

all together (in a group)
altogether (completely)

already (previous)
all ready (all are ready)

allowed (permitted)
aloud (audible)

altar (in a church)
alter (change)

ant (insect)
aunt (relative)

ante (before)
anti (against)

arc (part of a circle)
ark (boat)

ascent (climb)
assent (agree)

assistance (help)
assistants (those who help)

ate (did eat)
eight (number)

attendance (presence)
attendants (escorts)

aural (by ear)
oral (by mouth)

away (gone)
aweigh (clear anchor)

awful (terrible)
offal (entrails)

aye (yes)
eye (organ of sight)
I (pronoun)

bail (throw water out)
bale (bundle)

bait (lure)
bate (to decrease)

ball (round object)
bawl (cry)

band (plays music)
banned (forbidden)

bard (poet)
barred (having bars)

bare (nude)
bear (animal)

bark (dog's sound)
barque (ship)

baron (nobleman)
barren (no fruit)

base (lower part)
bass (deep tone)

based (at a base)
baste (cover with liquid)

bases (plural of base)
basis (foundation)

bask (warm feeling)
Basque (country)

bazaar (market)
bizarre (old)

be (exist)
bee (insect)

beach (shore)
beech (tree)

bearing (manner, machine)
baring (uncovering)

beat (whip)
beet (vegetable)

beau (boyfriend)
bow (decorative knot)

been (past participle of be)
bin (box)

beer (drink)
bier (coffin)

bell (something you ring)
belle (pretty woman)

berry (fruit)
bury (put in ground)

berth (bunk)
birth (born)

better (more good)
bettor (one who bets)

bight (slack part of rope)
bite (chew)
byte (computer unit)

billed (did bill)
build (construct)

blew (did blow)
blue (color]

block (cube)
bloc (group)

boar (hog)
bore (drill; be tiresome)

boarder (one who boards)
border (boundary)

bole (part of tree)
bowl (dish; game)

bolder (more bold)
boulder (big stone)

born (delivered at birth)
borne (carried)

borough (town)
burro (donkey)
burrow (dig)

bough (of a tree)
bow (of a ship)

bouillon (clear broth)
bullion (gold or silver)

boy (male child)
buoy (floating object)

brake (stop)
break (smash)

bread (food)
bred (cultivated)

brewed (steeped)
brood (flock)

brews (steeps)
bruise (sore on skin)

bridal (relating to bride)
bridle (headgear for horse)

Britain (country)
Briton (Englishman)

brooch (pin)
broach (bring up)

but (except)
butt (end)

buy (purchase)
by (near)
bye (farewell)

cache (hiding place)
cash (money)

callous (unfeeling)
callus (hard tissue)

cannon (big gun)
canon (law)

canvas (cloth)
canvass (survey)

capital (money; city)
Capitol (D.C. Congress)

carat (weight of stones)
caret (proofreader's mark)
carrot (vegetable)

carol (song)
carrel (study space in library)

cast (throw; actors in a play)
caste (social class)

cause (origin)
caws (crow calls)

cede (grant)
seed (part of a plant)

ceiling (top of room)
sealing (closing)

cell (prison room)
sell (exchange for money)

cellar (basement)
seller (one who sells)

censor (ban)
sensor (detection device)

cent (penny)
scent (odor)
sent (did send)

cereal (relating to grain)
serial (of a series)

cession (yielding)
session (meeting)

chance (luck)
chants (songs)

chased (did chase)
chaste (modest)

cheap (inexpensive)
cheep (bird call)

chews (bites)
choose (select)

chic (style)
sheik (Arab chief)

chilly (cold)
chili (hot pepper)

choir (singers)
quire (amount of paper)

choral (music)
coral (reef)

chorale (chorus)
corral (pen for livestock)

chord (musical notes)
cord (string)

chute (slide)
shoot (discharge gun)

cite (summon to court)
sight (see)
site (location)

claws (nails on animal's feet)
clause (part of a sentence)

click (small sound)
clique (exclusive subgroup)

climb (ascend)
clime (climate)

close (shut)
clothes (clothing)
cloze (test)

coal (fuel)
cole (cabbage)

coarse (rough)
course (path; subject)

colonel (military rank)
kernel (grain of corn)

complement (complete set)
compliment (praise)

coop (chicken pen)
coupe (car)

core (center)
corps (army group)

correspondence (letters)
correspondents (writers)

council (legislative body)
counsel (advise)

cousin (relative)
cozen (deceive)

creak (grating noise)
creek (stream)

crews (groups of workers)
cruise (sail)
cruse (small pot)

cruel (hurting)
crewel (stitching)

cue (prompt)
queue (line up)

currant (small raisin)
current (recent, fast stream)

curser (one who curses)
cursor (moving pointer)

cymbal (instrument)
symbol (sign)

deer (animal)
dear (greeting; loved one)

desert (abandon; dry place)
dessert (final part of meal)

die (expire)
dye (color)

dine (eat)
dyne (unit of force)

disburse (payout)
disperse (scatter)

discreet (unobtrusive)
discrete (non-continuous)

doe (female deer)
dough (bread mixture)

do (musical note)
do (shall)

dew (moisture)
due (owed)

done (finished)
dun (demand for payment;
     dull color)

dual (two)
duel (formal combat)

duct (tube)
ducked (did duck)

earn (work for)
urn (container)

ewe (female sheep)
yew (shrub)
you (personal pronoun)

eyelet (small hole)
islet (small island)

fain (gladly)
feign (pretend)

faint (weak)
feint (pretend attack)

fair (honest; bazaar)
fare (cost of transportation)

fawn (baby deer)
faun (mythical creature)

faze (upset)
phase (stage)

feat (accomplishment)
feet (plural of foot)

find (discover)
fined (penalty of money)

fir (tree)
fur (animal covering)

flair (talent)
flare (flaming signal)

flea (insect)
flee (run away)

flew (did fly)
flu (influenza)
flue (shaft)

flour (milled grain)
flower (bloom)

for (in favor of)
fore (front part)
four (number 4)

foreword (preface)
forward (front part)

forth (forward)
fourth (after third)

foul (bad)
fowl (bird)

franc (French money)
frank (honest)

freeze (cold)
frees (to free)
frieze (sculptured border)

friar (brother, religious order)
fryer (for cooking)

gate (fence opening)
gait (foot movement)

gilt (golden)
guilt (opposite of innocence)

gnu (antelope)
knew (did know)
new (opposite of old)

gorilla (animal)
guerrilla (irregular soldier)

grate (grind)
great (large)

groan (moan)
grown (cultivated)

guessed (surmised)
guest (company)

hail (ice; salute)
hale (healthy)

hair (on head)
hare (rabbit)

hall (passage)
haul (carry)

handsome (attractive)
hansom (carriage)

hangar (storage building)
hanger (to hang things on)

halve (cut in half)
have (possess)

hart (deer)
heart (body organ)

hay (dried grass)
hey (expression for attention)

heal (make well)
heel (bottom of foot)
he'll (he will)

hear (listen)
here (this place)

heard (listened)
herd (group of animals)

heed (pay attention)
he'd (he would)

hertz (wave frequency)
hurts (pain)

hew (carve)
hue (colour)

hi (hello)
hie (hasten)
high (opposite of low)

higher (above)
hire (employ)

him (pronoun)
hymn (religious song)

hoarse (husky voice)
horse (animal)

hole (opening)
whole (complete)

holey (full of holes)
holy (sacred)
wholly (all)

horde (crowd)
hoard (hidden supply)

hostel (lodging for youth)
hostile (unfriendly)

hour (sixty minutes)
our (possessive pronoun)

hurdle (jump over)
hurtle (throw)

idle (lazy)
idol (false god)
idyll (charming scene)

in (opposite of out)
inn (hotel)

insight (self-knowledge)
incite (cause)

instance (example)
instants (periods of time)

insure (protect against loss)
ensure (make sure)

intense (extreme)
intents (aims)

jam (fruit jelly)
jamb (window part)

knit (weave with yarn)
nit (louse egg)

lam (escape)
lamb (baby sheep)

lain (past participle of lie)
lane (narrow way)

lay (recline)
lei (necklace of flowers)

lead (metal)
led (guided)

leak (crack)
leek (vegetable)

lean (slender; incline)
lien (claim)

leased (rented)
least (smallest)

lessen (make less)
lesson (instruction)

levee (embankment)
levy (impose legally)

liar (untruthful)
lyre (musical instrument)

lichen (fungus)
liken (compare)

lie (falsehood)
lye (alkaline solution)

lieu (instead of)
Lou (name)

lightening (become light)
lightning (weather element)

load (burden)
lode (vein or ore)

loan (something borrowed)
lone (single)

locks (plural of lock)
lox (smoked salmon)

loot (steal)
lute (musical instrument)

low (not high; cattle sound)
lo (interjection)

made (manufactured)
maid (servant)

mail (send by post)
male (masculine)

main (most important)
Maine (state)
mane (hair)

maize (Indian corn)
maze (confusing path)

mall (courtyard; shops)
maul (attack)

manner (style)
manor (estate)

mantel (over fireplace)
mantle (cloak)

marry (join together)
merry (joyful)
Mary (name)

marshal (escort)
martial (militant)

massed (grouped)
mast (support)

maybe (perhaps, adj.)
may be (is possible, v.)

meat (beef)
meet (greet)
mete (measure)

medal (award)
meddle (interfere)

might (may; strength)
mite (small insect)

miner (coal digger)
minor (juvenile)

missed (failed to attain)
mist (fog)

moan (groan)
mown (cut down)

mode (fashion)
mowed (cut down)

morn (early day)
mourn (grieve)

muscle (flesh)
mussel (shellfish)

naval (nautical)
navel (dip on abdomen)

nay (no)
neigh (whinny)

need (require)
knead (mix with hands)

new (not old)
knew (remembered)
gnu (animal)

night (evening)
knight (feudal warrior)

no (negative)
know (familiar with)

none (not any)
nun (religious sister)

not (in no manner)
knot (tangle)

oar (of a boat)
or (conjunction)
ore (mineral deposit)

ode (poem)
owed (did owe)

oh (exclamation)
owe (be indebted)

one (number)
won (triumphed)

overdo (go to extremes)
overdue (past due)

overseas (abroad)
oversees (supervises)

pail (bucket)
pale (white)

pain (discomfort)
pane (window glass)

pair (two of a kind)
pare (peel)
pear (fruit)

palate (roof of mouth)
palette (board for paint)
pallet (tool)

passed (went by)
past (former)

patience (composure)
patients (sick persons)

pause (brief stop)
paws (feet of animals)

peace (tranquility)
piece (part)

peak (mountaintop)
peek (look)
pique (offense)

peal (ring)
peel (pare)

pearl (jewel)
purl (knitting stitch)

pedal (ride a bike)
peddle (sell)

peer (equal)
pier (dock)

per (for each)
purr (cat sound)

pi (Greek letter)
pie (kind of pastry)

plain (simple)
plane (flat surface; aircraft)

plait (braid)
plate (dish)

pleas (plural of plea)
please (to be agreeable)

plum (fruit)
plumb (lead weight)

pole (stick)
poll (vote)

pore (ponder; skin gland)
pour (flow freely)

pray (worship)
prey (victim)

presents (gifts)
presence (appearance)

principal (chief)
principle (rule)

profit (benefit)
prophet (seer)

rack (framework; torture)
wrack (ruin)

rain (precipitation)
reign (royal authority)
rein (harness)

raise (put up)
raze (tear down)
rays (of sun)

rap (hit; talk)
wrap (cover)

read (peruse)
reed (plant)
read (perused)
red (color)

real (genuine)
reel (spool)

reek (give off strong odor)
wreak (inflict)

rest (relax)
wrest (force)

review (look back)
revue (musical)

right (correct)
rite (ceremony)
write (inscribe)

rime (ice, or rhyme)
rhyme (same end sound)

ring (circular band)
wring (squeeze)

road (street)
rode (transported)
rowed (used oars)

roe (fish eggs)
row (line; use oars)

role (character)
roll (turn over; bread)

root (part of a plant)
route (highway)

rose (flower; arise)
rows (lines)

rote (by memory)
wrote (did write)

rude (impolite)
rued (was sorry)

rumor (gossip)
roomer (renter)

rung (step on a ladder; past tense of ring)
wrung (squeezed)

rye (grain)
wry (twisted)

sail (travel by boat)
sale (bargain)

scene (setting)
seen (viewed)

scull (boat; row)
skull (head)

sea (ocean)
see (visualize)

seam (joining mark)
seem (appear to be)

sear (singe)
seer (prophet)

serf (feudal servant)
surf (waves)

sew (mend)
so (in order that)
sow (plant)

shear (cut)
sheer (transparent)

shoe (foot covering)
shoo (drive away)

shoot (use gun)
chute (trough)

shone (beamed)
shown (exhibited)

side (flank)
sighed (audible breath)

sign (signal)
sine (trigonometric function)

slay (kill)
sleigh (sled)

sleight (dexterity)
slight (slender)

slew (killed)
slue (swamp)

soar (fly)
sore (painful)

sole (only)
soul (spirit)

some (portion)
sum (total)

son (male offspring)
sun (star)

staid (proper)
stayed (remained)

stair (step)
stare (look intently)

stake (post)
steak (meat)

stationary (fixed; unmoving)
stationery (paper)

steal (rob)
steel (metal)

step (walk)
steppe (prairie– Europe/Asia)

stile (gate)
style (fashion)

straight (not crooked)
strait (channel of water)

suite (connected rooms)
sweet (sugary)

surge (sudden increase)
serge (fabric; outfit)

tacks (plural of tack)
tax (assess; burden)

tail (animal's appendage)
tale (story)

taught (did teach)
taut (tight)

tea (drink)
tee (holder for golf ball)

teas (plural of tea)
tease (mock)

team (crew)
teem (be full)

tear (cry)
tier (level)

tear (rip apart)
tare (weight deduction)

tern (sea bird)
turn (rotate)

their (possessive pronoun)
there (at that place)
they're (they are)

theirs (possessive pronoun)
there's (there is)

threw (tossed)
through (finished)

throne (king's seat)
thrown (tossed)

thyme (herb)
time (duration)

tic (twitch)
tick (insect; sound of clock)

tide (ebb and flow)
tied (bound)

to (toward)
too (also)
two (number)

toad (frog)
towed (pulled)

toe (digit on foot)
tow (pull)

told (informed)
tolled (rang)

trussed (tied)
trust (confidence)

vain (conceited)
vane (wind indicator)
vein (blood vessel)

vale (valley)
veil (face cover)

vary (change)
very (absolutely)

vice (bad habit
vise (clamp)

vile (disgusting)
vial (small bottle)

wade (walk in water)
weighed (measured weight)

wail (cry)
whale (sea mammal)

waist (middle)
waste (trash; use poorly)

wait (linger)
weight (heaviness)

waive (forgive)
wave (swell)

want (desire)
wont (custom)

ware (pottery)
wear (have on)
where (what place)

way (road; means)
weigh (measure heaviness)
whey (watery part of milk)

ways (way plural; shipyard)
weighs (heaviness)

we (pronoun)
wee (small)

weak (not strong)
week (seven days)

weal (prosperity)
we'll (we will)
wheel (circular frame)

weather (atmosphere state)
whether (if)

weave (interlace)
we've (we have)

we'd (we would)
weed (plant)

weir (dam)
we're (we are)

wet (moist)
whet (sharpen)

which (what one)
witch (sorceress)

while (during)
wile (trick)

whine (complaining sound)
wine (drink)

who's (who is)
whose (possessive of who)

wood (of a tree)
would (is willing to)

yoke (harness)
yolk (egg center)

you (pronoun)
ewe (female sheep)
yew (evergreen tree)

you'll (you will)
yule (Christmas)

your (possessive pronoun)
you're (you are)

EASILY-CONFUSED WORDS (& MEANINGS)

The following groups of words are frequently used incorrectly. Some are confused because they sound the same but have different meanings; others look and sound different from each other but have meanings that are related. Even those of us who understand these words make mistakes when we are in a hurry.

accede (v.)-to comply with
exceed (v.)-to surpass

accent (n.)-stress in speech or writing
ascent (n.)-act of going up
assent (v., n.)-consent

accept (v.)-to agree or take what is offered
except (prep.)-leaving out or excluding

access (n.)-admittance
excess (n., adj.)-surplus

adapt (v.)-to adjust
adept (adj.)-proficient
adopt (v.)-to take by choice

adverse (adj.)-opposing
averse (adj.)-disinclined

affect (v.)-feeling
effect (n.)-consequence or result

alley (n.)-narrow street
ally (n.)-supporter

allusion (n.)-indirect reference
delusion (n.)-mistaken belief
illusion (n.)-mistaken vision, not real

all ready (adj.)-completely ready
already (adv.)-even now or by this time

all together (pron., adj.)-everything/everyone in one
                place
altogether (adv.)-entirely

anecdote (n.)-short amusing story
   antidote (n.)-something to counter the effect of poison

angel (n.)-heavenly body
angle (n.)-space between two lines that meet in a point

annul (v.)-to make void
annual (adj.)-yearly

ante -prefix meaning before
anti -prefix meaning against

any way (adj., n.)-in whatever manner
anyway (adv.] -regardless

appraise (v.)-to set a value on
apprise (v.)-to inform

area (n.)-surface
aria (n.)-melody

biannual (adj.)-occurring twice per year
biennial (adj.)-occurring every other year

bibliography (n.)-list of writings on a particular topic,
            references
biography (n.)-written history of a person's life

bizarre (adj.)-odd
bazaar (n.)-market, fair

breadth (n.)-width
breath (n.)-respiration
breathe (v.)-to inhale and exhale

calendar (n.)-chart of days and months
colander (n.)-a strainer

casual (adj.)-informal
causal (adj.)=-relating to cause

catch (v.)-to grab
ketch (n.)-type of boat

cease (v.)-to stop
seize (v.) -to grasp

click (n.)-short, sharp sound
clique (n.)-small exclusive subgroup

collision (n.)-a clashing
collusion (n.)-a scheme to cheat

coma (n.)-an unconscious state
comma (n.)-a punctuation mark

command (n.,v.)-an order, to order
commend (v.)-to praise, to entrust

comprehensible (adj.) -understandable
comprehensive (adj.)-extensive

confidant (n.)-friend or advisor
confident (adj.)-sure

confidentially (adv.)-privately
confidently (adv.)-certainly

conscience (n.)-sense of right and wrong
conscious (adj.)-c-aware

contagious (adj.)-spread by contact
contiguous (adj.)-touching or nearby

continual (adj.)-repeated, happening again and again
continuous (adj.)-uninterrupted, without stopping

cooperation (n.)-the art of working together
corporation (n.)-a business organization

costume (n.)-special way of dressing
custom (n.)-usual practice of habit

council (n.)-an official group
counsel (v.)-to give advice
counsel (n.)-advice

credible (adj.)-believable
creditable (adj.)-deserving praise

deceased (adj.)-dead
diseased (adj.)-ill

decent (adj.)-proper
descent (n.)-way down
dissent (n., v)-disagreement, to disagree

deference (n.) -respect
difference (n.) -dissimilarity

deposition (n.)-a formal written document
disposition (n.)-temperament

depraved (adj.)-morally corrupt
deprived (adj.)-taken away from

deprecate (v.)-to disapprove
depreciate (v.)-to lessen in value

desert (n.)-arid land
desert (v.)-to abandon
dessert (n.)-course served at the end of a meal

desolate (adj.)-lonely, sad
dissolute (adj.)-loose in morals

detract (v.)-to take away from
distract (v.)-to divert attention away from

device (n.)-a contrivance
devise (v.)-to plan

disapprove (v.)-to withhold approval
disprove (v.)-to prove something to be false

disassemble (v.)-to take something apart
dissemble (v.)-to disguise

disburse (v.)-to pay out
disperse (v.)-to scatter

discomfort (n.)-distress, not comfortable
discomfit (v.)-to frustrate or embarrass

disinterested (adj.)-impartial
uninterested (adj.)-not interested

effect (n.)-result of a cause
effect (v.)-to make happen

elapse (v.)-to pass
lapse (v.)-to become void
relapse (v.)-to fall back to previous condition

elicit (v.)-to draw out
illicit (adj.)-unlawful

eligible (adj.)-ready
illegible (adj.)-can't be read

elusive (adj.)-hard to catch
illusive (adj.)-misleading

eminent (adj.)-well known
imminent (adj.)-c-impending

emerge (v.)-rise out of
Immerge (v.)-plunge into

emigrate (v.)-to leave a country and take up residence elsewhere
immigrate (v.)-to enter a country for the purpose of taking up residence

envelop (v.)-to surround
envelope (n.)-a wrapper for a letter

erasable (adj.)-capable of being erased
irascible (adj.)-c-easily provoked to anger

expand (v.)-to increase in size
expend (v.)-to spend

expect (v.)-to suppose; to look forward
suspect (v.)-to mistrust

extant (adj.)-still existing
extent (n.)-amount

facility (n.)-ease
felicity (n.)-happiness

farther (adj.)-more distant (refers to space)
further (adj.)-extending beyond a point (refers to time, quantity, or degree)

finale (n.)-the end
finally (adv.)-at the end
finely (adv.)-in a fine manner

fiscal (adj.)-relating to finance
physical (adj.)-relating to the body

formally (adv. Adv.) with rigid ceremony
formerly (adv.)-previously

human (adj.)-relating to mankind
humane (adv.)-kind

hypercritical (adj.)-very critical
hypocritical (adj.)-pretending to be virtuous

imitate (v.)-to mimic
intimate (v.)-to hint or make known; familiar, close

incredible (adj.)-too extraordinary to be believed
incredulous (adj.)-unbelieving, sceptical

indigenous (adj.)-native
indigent (adj.)-needy
indignant (adj.)-angry

21

infer (v.)-to arrive at by reason
imply (v.)-to suggest meaning indirectly

ingenious (adj.)-clever
ingenuous (adj.)- straightforward

later (adj.)-more late
latter (adj.)-second in a series of two

lay (v.)-to set something down or place something
lie (v.) - to recline

least (adj.)-at the minimum
lest (conj.)-for fear that

lend (v.)-to give for a time
loan (n.)-received to use for a time

loose (adj.)-not tight
lose (v.)-not win; misplace

magnet (n.)-iron bar with power to attract iron
magnate (n.)-person in prominent position in large
          industry

message (n.)-communication
massage (v.)-rub body

moral (n., adj.)-lesson; ethic
morale (n.)-mental condition

morality (n.)-virtue
mortality (n.)-the state of being mortal; death rate

of (prep.)-having to do with; indicating possession
off (adv.)-not on

official (adj.)-authorized
officious (adj.)-offering services where they are neither
wanted nor needed

oral (adj.)-verbal
aural (adj.)-listening

pasture (n.)-grass field
pastor (n.)-minister

perfect (adj.)-without fault
prefect {n.)-an official

perpetrate (v.)-to be guilty of; to commit
perpetuate (v)-to make perpetual

22

perquisite (n.)-a privilege or profit in addition to salary
prerequisite (n.)-a preliminary requirement

persecute (v.)-to harass, annoy, or injure
prosecute (v.)-to press for punishment of crime

personal (adj.)-private
personnel (n)-people employed in an organization

peruse (v.)-to read
pursue (v.)-to follow in order to overtake

picture (n.)-drawing or photograph
pitcher (n.)-container for liquid; baseball player

precede (v.)-to go before
proceed (v.)-to advance

preposition (n.)-a part of speech
proposition (n.)-a proposal or suggestion

pretend (v.)-to make believe
portend (v.)-to give a sign of something that will happen

quiet (adj.)-not noisy
quit (v.)-to stop
quite (adv.)-very

recent (adj.)-not long ago
resent (v.)-to feel indignant

respectably (adv.)-in a respectable manner
respectively (adv.)-in order indicated
respectfully (adv.)-in a respectful manner

restless (adj.)-constantly moving, uneasy
restive (adj.)-contrary, resisting control

suppose (v.)-assume or imagine
supposed (adj.)-expected

than (conj.)-used in comparison
then (adv.)-at that time; next in order of time

through (prep.)-by means of; beginning to end
thorough (adj.)-complete

use (v.)-employ something
used (adj.)-second hand

veracious (adj.)-truthful
vivacious (adj.)-attractive, lively, animated
voracious (adj.)-greedy

ENGLISH TERMS TO KNOW – BY GRADE
INDEX OF TERMS

Terms are listed here in alphabetical order and by both page and grade numbers.

Term	Grade	Page
Active Voice	11	55
Allegory	10	46
Alliteration	8	31
Allusion	9	39
Analogy	10	46
Anecdotal Evidence	11	55
Antagonist	8	31
Anti-climax	10	46
Antithesis	11	55
Aphorism	11	55
Apostrophe	11	55
Archaic language	10	46
Argumentative Essay	10	46
Aside	10	47
Assonance	8	31
Atmosphere	9	39
Audience	9	39
Autobiography	9	39
Ballad Stanza	9	39
Ballad	9	39
Bias	9	39
Biography	9	40
Blank verse	9	40
Cacophony	11	56
Caricature	10	47
Case Study	10	47
Catastrophe	10	47
Cause and Effect	10	47
Character Foil	9	40

Character	8	31
Characterization	9	40
Chorus	10	47
Chronological Order	10	47
Cliché	9	40
Climactic Order	10	47
Climax	8	31
Colloquialism / C. Language	10	48
Comedy	8	31
Comic Relief	10	48
Compare and Contrast	9	40
Comparison	8	32
Conflict	8	32
Connotation	9	40
Consonance	8	32
Contrast	8	32
Couplet	8	32
Denotation	9	41
Denouement / Resolution	9	41
Descriptive Essay	10	48
Dialect	9	41
Dialogue	8	32
Diary	8	32
Diction	10	48
Didactic	11	56
Dilemma	9	41
Direct Presentation	9	41
Dissonance	11	56
Drama	9	41
Dramatic Form	11	56
Dramatic Irony	10	48
Dramatic Monologue	10	48
Dynamic Character	9	41
Editorial	11	56
Elegy	10	49
Emotional Appeal	10	49
Epic	10	49

26

Epigram	10	49
Epilogue	10	49
Epiphany	10	49
Epitaph	10	49
Euphemism	11	56
Euphony	11	57
Expert Testimony	11	57
Exposition	10	50
Expository Essay	9	42
Extended Metaphor	10	50
External Conflict	8	33
Fable	8	33
Falling Action	8	33
Fantasy	8	33
Farce	12	60
Figurative Language	9	42
First Person Point of View	8	33
Flashback	8	33
Flat Character	9	42
Foil / Character Foil	10	50
Foreshadowing	8	33
Form	9	42
Formal Essay	10	50
Formal Language	9	42
Frame Story	11	57
Free verse	8	34
Genre	8	34
Graphic text / Graphic Novel	9	42
Hero / Heroine	8	34
Historical Reference	9	42
Hyperbole	8	34
Iambic Pentameter	10	50
Idiom	9	43
Image	8	34
Imagery	8	34
Indeterminate Ending	10	50
Indirect presentation	9	43

Informal Essay	10	51
Informal Language	9	43
Interior Monologue	11	57
Internal Conflict	8	34
Internal Rhyme	9	43
Irony	10	51
Jargon	9	43
Juxtaposition	10	51
Legend	8	34
Limited Omniscient P.O.V.	9	43
Literal Language	11	57
Lyric	10	51
Melodrama	12	60
Metaphor	8	35
Metre	10	51
Monologue	10	52
Mood	9	43
Mystery	9	44
Myth	8	35
Narration	8	35
Narrative	9	44
Narrator	8	35
Objective (language tone etc.)	10	52
Objective Point of View	9	44
Octave	11	57
Ode	10	52
Omniscient Point of View	9	44
Onomatopoeia	8	35
Oxymoron	10	52
Paradox	10	52
Parallelism	11	58
Parody	11	58
Passive Voice	11	58
Pastoral	12	60
Pathos	10	52
Personal Essay	9	44
Personification	8	35

Persuasive Essay	10	53
Persuasive Technique	11	58
Plot	8	35
Point of view	8	35
Pro and Con Argument	9	45
Prologue	10	53
Propaganda	9	44
Protagonist	8	36
Proverb	9	44
Pun	9	45
Purpose	8	36
Quatrain	10	53
Question and answer	8	36
Refrain	8	36
Repetition	8	36
Research	8	36
Resolution	8	36
Rhetorical Question	9	45
Rhyme Scheme	8	37
Rhyme	8	37
Rhythm	9	45
Rising Action	8	37
Round Character	9	45
Sarcasm	10	53
Satire	10	53
Sestet	11	58
Setting	8	37
Simile	8	37
Slang	8	37
Soliloquy	10	53
Sonnet	10	53
Speaker	8	37
Stanza	8	37
Static Character	10	54
Statistical Evidence	11	58
Stereotype	8	37
Stock / Stereotyped Character	10	54

Story within a Story	11	59
Stream of Consciousness	11	59
Style	11	59
Stylistic Technique	12	60
Subjective (language tone)	11	59
Surprise Ending	9	45
Suspense	8	38
Symbol / Symbolism	10	54
Theme	8	38
Thesis statement	8	38
Thesis	8	38
Third person point of view	8	38
Tone	8	38
Tragedy	10	54
Understatement	10	54
Voice	10	55
Wit	11	59

ENGLISH TERMS TO KNOW – BY GRADE

The following literary terms should be known through each grade level. By grade 12, students should be familiar with all terms provided here.

Know the following in Grade 8

Alliteration
The repetition of initial sounds in neighboring words; e.g. "And sings a solitary song That whistles in the wind."

Antagonist
The character who opposes the hero, or protagonist. The antagonist, when there is one, provides the story's conflict.

Assonance
The repetition of vowel sounds to create internal rhyming within phrases or sentences, and together with alliteration and consonance serves as one of the building blocks of verse.

Character
A person depicted in a narrative or drama. Characters may be flat, minor characters; or round, and major. The main character in a story is generally known as the protagonist; the character who opposes him or her is the antagonist.

Climax
A decisive moment that is of maximum intensity or is a major turning point in a plot.

Comedy
A dramatic work that is often (but need not be) light, humorous or satirical in tone and that contains a happy resolution to the thematic conflict.

Comparison

The act of finding out the differences and similarities between two or more people or things.

Conflict

A literary element that involves a struggle between two opposing forces usually a protagonist and an antagonist. The primary categories of conflict are man vs man / society / nature / self / supernatural.

Consonance

A poetic device characterized by the repetition of the same consonant two or more times in short succession, as in "pitter patter" or in "all mammals named Sammy are clammy."

Contrast

A device where two objects or ideas are put in opposition to one another to show or emphasize the differences between them.

Couplet

A unit of verse consisting of two successive lines, usually rhyming and having the same meter and often forming a complete thought or syntactic unit.

Dialogue

The conversation between characters in a novel, drama, etc.

Diary

A form of autobiographical writing, a regularly kept record of the diarist's activities and reflections. Written primarily for the writer's use alone, the diary has a frankness that is unlike writing done for publication.

External Conflict
Struggle between a literary or dramatic character and an outside force such as nature or another character, which drives the dramatic action of the plot.

Fable
A fictional story, in prose or verse, that features animals, mythical creatures, plants, inanimate objects or forces of nature which are given human qualities such as speech, and that illustrates or leads to an interpretation of a moral lesson.

Falling Action
The part of a literary plot that occurs after the climax has been reached and the conflict has been resolved.

Fantasy
A genre of fiction that commonly uses magic and other supernatural phenomena as a primary plot element, theme, or setting. Many works within the genre take place in imaginary worlds where magic and magical creatures are common.

Flashback
A narrative technique that allows a writer to present past events during current events, in order to provide background for the current narration. By giving material that occurred prior to the present event, the writer provides the reader with insight into a character's motivation and or background to a conflict.

First Person Point of View
The story is told in first person, with a narrator who is a character in the story. Readers can get into only the narrator's thoughts to know what she or he is thinking about the action or other characters in the story.

Foreshadowing
A literary device in which a writer gives an advance hint of what is to come later in the story.

Free verse
Verse composed of variable, usually unrhymed lines having no fixed metrical pattern.

Genre
A category of literary composition. Genres may be determined by literary technique, tone, content, or even (as in the case of fiction) length.

Hero / Heroine
The main character in a literary work. The term is also used in a specialized sense for any figure celebrated in the ancient legends of a people or in such early heroic epics as *the Iliad, Beowulf,* or *The Song of Roland.*

Hyperbole
A figure of speech in which exaggeration is used for emphasis or effect; e.g. *"I could sleep for a year"* or *"This book weighs a ton."*

Image
A mental picture or association of ideas evoked in a literary work, especially in poetry.

Imagery
The use of vivid or figurative language to represent objects, actions, or ideas.

Internal Conflict
Psychological struggle within the mind of a literary or dramatic character, the resolution of which creates the plot's suspense.

Legend
A non-historical or unverifiable story handed down by tradition from earlier times and popularly accepted as historical.

Metaphor
A figure of speech in which a term or phrase is applied to something to which it is not literally applicable in order to suggest a resemblance, as in "A mighty fortress is our God."

Myth
A traditional, typically ancient story dealing with supernatural beings, ancestors, or heroes.

Narration
A recital of events, especially in chronological order, as the story narrated in a poem or the exposition in a drama.

Narrator
A person who gives an account or tells the story of events, experiences, etc.

Onomatopoeia
Words whose very sound is very close to the sound they are meant to depict; e.g. grunt, huff, buzz and snap.

Personification
A figure of speech in which inanimate objects or abstractions are endowed with human qualities or are represented as possessing human form, as in *Hunger sat shivering on the road* or *Flowers danced about the lawn.*

Plot
Also called storyline. The plan, scheme, or main story of a literary or dramatic work, as a play, novel, or short story.

Point of view
The position of the narrator in relation to the story, as indicated by the narrator's outlook from which the events are depicted and by the attitude toward the characters.

Protagonist
The main character in a story, novel, drama, or other literary work, the character that the reader or audience empathizes with.

Purpose
In composition, a person's reason for writing, such as to inform, entertain, explain, or persuade.

Question and answer
A problem for discussion or under discussion; a matter for investigation.

Refrain
A line or set of lines at the end of a stanza or section of a longer poem or song--these lines repeat at regular intervals in other stanzas or sections of the same work. Sometimes the repetition involves minor changes in wording.

Repetition
The simple repeating of a word, within a sentence or a poetical line, with no particular placement of the words, in order to provide emphasis.

Research
The systematic investigation into and study of materials and sources in order to establish facts and reach new conclusions.

Resolution
The part of a literary work in which the complications of the plot are resolved or simplified.

Rhyme
A poem or verse having a regular correspondence of sounds, especially at the ends of lines. A word that corresponds with another in terminal sound, as *behold* and *cold*.

Rhyme Scheme
The pattern of rhyme in a poem, often symbolized by letters, such as *ab ab* or *abbc abbc*.

Rising Action
The events of a dramatic or narrative plot preceding the climax.

Setting
The location and time frame in which the action of a narrative takes place.

Simile
A figure of speech in which two unlike things are compared, using "like" or "as", as in "she is like a rose." Similar to a Metaphor, except a metaphor does not use "like" or "as."

Slang
A type of language that consists of words and phrases that are regarded as very informal, are more common in speech than writing, and are typically restricted to a particular context or group of people.

Speaker
The voice in a poem or the narrator of the story. The speaker may be the poet or a character created by the poet. The speaker may also be a thing or an animal that tells the story to the audience.

Stanza
One of the divisions of a poem, composed of two or more lines usually characterized by a common pattern of meter, rhyme, and number of lines.

Stereotype
A character who is so ordinary or unoriginal that the character seems like an oversimplified representation of a type, gender, class, religious group, or occupation.

Suspense
That quality of a literary work that makes the reader or audience uncertain or tense about the outcome of events. Suspense makes the reader ask "What will happen next?". Suspense is greatest when it focuses attention on a sympathetic character.

Theme
The central idea or ideas explored by a literary work. It is not the same as a moral. Theme is an overarching generalization about life or the world, not tied to the original story; e.g. "The drive for power may corrupt good men."

Thesis
A proposition stated or put forward for consideration, especially one to be discussed and proved or to be maintained against objections. It is normally the subject or purpose for an essay.

Thesis statement
A short statement, usually a 15 to 25 word sentence, that summarizes the main point or claim of an essay, search paper, etc., and is developed, supported, and explained in the text by means of examples and evidence.

Third person point of view
A form of storytelling in which a narrator relates all action in third person, using third person pronouns such as "he" or "she." Third person point of view may be omniscient or limited.

Tone
A literary technique which encompasses the attitudes toward the subject and toward the audience implied in a literary work, play, or film.

Know the following (and all previous) in Grade 9

Allusion
A brief reference to a person, event, or place, real or fictitious, or to a work of art. Casual reference to a famous historical or literary figure or event. An allusion may be drawn from history, geography, literature, or religion.

Atmosphere
The pervading tone or mood of a place, situation, or work of art.

Audience
The person(s) reading a text, listening to a speaker, or observing a performance. The person(s) for whom a work is intended.

Autobiography
A non-fictional account of a person's life--usually a celebrity, an important historical figure, or a writer--written by that actual person.

Ballad
a poem or song narrating a story in short stanzas. Traditional ballads are typically of unknown authorship, having been passed on orally from one generation to the next as part of the folk culture.

Ballad Stanza
A stanza consisting of four lines with the first and third lines unrhymed iambic tetrameters and the second and fourth lines rhymed iambic trimeters.

Bias
prejudice in favor of or against one thing, person, or group compared with another, usually in a way considered to be unfair.

Biography
An account of someone's life written by someone else.

Blank verse
Poetry written in regular metrical but unrhymed lines, almost always iambic pentameters.

Characterization
The method used by a writer to develop a character. The method includes showing the character's appearance, displaying the character's actions or thoughts, letting the character speak, and getting the reactions of others.

Character Foil
A character who contrasts with another character (usually the protagonist) in order to highlight particular qualities of the other character. A foil usually either differs drastically or is extremely similar but with a key difference setting them apart.

Cliché
A trite, stereotyped expression; a sentence or phrase, usually expressing a popular or common thought or idea, that has lost originality, ingenuity, and impact by long overuse, as "sadder but wiser," or "strong as an ox."

Compare and Contrast (essays / writing)
A comparison essay is an essay in which you emphasize the similarities, and a contrast essay is an essay in which you emphasize the differences. We use comparison and contrast thinking when deciding which university to attend, which smartphone to buy, or whether to vacation at home or abroad.

Connotation
An idea or feeling that a word invokes in addition to its literal or primary meaning.

Denotation
The literal meaning or definition of a word.

Denouement / Resolution
The events following the climax and falling action of a drama or novel, in which a resolution or clarification takes place.

Dialect
The language used by the people of a specific area, class, district or any other group of people. It involves the spelling, sounds, grammar and pronunciation used by a particular group, and it distinguishes them from other people around them.

Dilemma
A situation in which a character must choose between two courses of action, both undesirable.

Direct Presentation
The writer tells readers what kind of personality the character possesses rather than allowing the character to show his or her personality and allow readers to draw their own conclusions.

Drama
A composition in prose or verse presenting in dialogue or pantomime a story involving conflict or contrast of character, especially one intended to be acted on the stage; a play.

Dynamic Character
A literary or dramatic character who undergoes an important inner change, as a change in personality or attitude. The character is not the same person he/she was at the outset.

Expository Essay
A genre of essay that requires the student to investigate an idea, evaluate evidence, expound on the idea, and set forth an argument concerning that idea in a clear and concise manner. This can be accomplished through comparison and contrast, definition, example, the analysis of cause and effect, etc.

Figurative Language
Speech or writing that departs from literal meaning in order to achieve a special effect or meaning, often using simile and metaphor.

Flat Character
A literary character whose personality can be defined by one or two traits and does not change in the course of the story.

Form
The "shape" or organizational mode of a particular poem. In most poems (like sonnets), the form consists of a set number of lines, a set rhyme scheme, and a set meter for each line.

Formal Language
The words which seem most suitable to the purpose and audience. In academic writing, writers use formal language and avoid the use of slang and colloquial language.

Graphic text / Graphic Novel
A combination of words and pictures to tell a story.

Historical Reference
A reference to some event, person, or significant theme from the past.

Idiom
A speech form or an expression of a given language that is peculiar to itself grammatically or cannot be understood from the individual meanings of its elements. It is often not understood outside a set language or cultural group; e.g. "It is raining cats and dogs" or "The pen ran out of ink."

Indirect presentation
The writer presents the character in action, allowing the reader to draw his or her own conclusions about the personality of that character.

Informal Language
A broad term for speech or writing marked by a casual, familiar, and generally colloquial use of language.

Internal Rhyme
A practice of forming a rhyme in only one lone line of verse. Ie: "We were the first that ever burst."

Jargon
Several possible meanings: 1) The specialized or technical language of a trade, profession, or similar group. 2) Speech or writing having unusual or pretentious vocabulary, convoluted phrasing, and vague meaning. 3) Nonsensical, incoherent, or meaningless talk.

Limited Omniscient Point of View
The narrator of the story can see and know all for a certain part of the story or for certain characters only.

Mood
One element in the narrative structure of a piece of literature. It can also be referred to as atmosphere because it creates an emotional setting enveloping the reader. Mood is established in order to affect the reader emotionally and psychologically and to provide a feeling for the narrative.

Mystery

A genre of fiction in which a detective, either an amateur or a professional, solves a crime or a series of crimes. Because detective stories rely on logic, supernatural elements rarely come into play.

Narrative

Some kind of retelling, often in words, of something that happened (a story).

Objective Point of View

The writer tells what happens without stating more than can be inferred from the story's action and dialogue.

Omniscient Point of View

A method of storytelling in which the narrator knows the thoughts and feelings of all of the characters in the story.

Personal Essay

Either a personal narrative in which the author writes about a personal incident or experience that provided significant personal meaning or a lesson learned, or it is a personal opinion about some topic or issue that is important to the writer.

Propaganda

A form of communication aimed towards influencing the attitude of the community toward some cause or position. Propaganda statements may be partly false and partly true. It is usually repeated and dispersed over a wide variety of media in order to create the chosen result in audience attitudes.

Proverb

a simple and concrete saying, popularly known and repeated, that expresses a truth based on common sense or the practical experience of humanity. They are often metaphorical.

Pro and Con Argument
The favorable and the unfavorable factors or reasons; advantages and disadvantages.

Pun
A joke or type of wordplay in which similar senses or sounds of two words or phrases, or different senses of the same word, are deliberately confused.
e.g. "Atheism is a non-prophet institution."

Rhetorical Question
A figure of speech in the form of a question that is asked in order to make a point. The question, a rhetorical device, is posed not to elicit a specific answer, but rather to encourage the listener to consider a message or viewpoint.

Rhythm
A literary device which demonstrates the long and short patterns through stressed and unstressed syllables particularly in verse form.

Round Character
A major character in a work of fiction who encounters conflict and is changed by it. Round characters tend to be more fully developed and described than flat, or static, characters.

Surprise Ending
An ending meant to shock the reader with an unexpected revelation or turn of events. These are most effective if, in hindsight, there was foreshadowing enough to suggest to upcoming twist. The strength of a surprise ending is based on the fairness by which it is achieved.

Allegory

A form of extended metaphor, in which objects, persons, and actions in a narrative, are equated with the meanings that lie outside the narrative itself. The underlying meaning has moral, social, religious, or political significance, and characters are often personifications of abstract ideas as charity, greed, or envy. Thus an allegory is a story with two meanings, a literal meaning and a symbolic meaning.

Analogy

A comparison in which the subject is compared point by point to something far different, usually with the idea of clarifying the subject by comparing it to something familiar. Analogies can provide insights and also imply that the similarities already present between the two subjects can mean even more; e.g. "Life is like a race." Or "How a doctor diagnoses diseases is like how a detective investigates crimes."

Anti-climax

A disappointing or ineffective conclusion to a series of events. Something preceded by significant events that has no comparable emotional or other payoff.

Argumentative essay / Persuasive essay

A genre of writing that requires the student to investigate a topic; collect, generate, and evaluate evidence; and establish a position on the topic in a concise manner.

Archaic language

Words and phrases that were used regularly in a language, but are now less common are archaic. Such words and phrases are often used deliberately to refer to earlier times.

Aside
A device in which a character in a drama makes a short speech which is heard by the audience, but not by other characters in the play.

Caricature
A representation in which the subject's distinctive features or peculiarities are deliberately exaggerated to produce a comic or grotesque effect.

Case Study
A descriptive, exploratory or explanatory analysis of a person, group or event with a view to making generalizations or over-arching conclusions.

Catastrophe
A sudden, extensive, or notable disaster or misfortune.

Cause and Effect
A method of paragraph or essay development in which a writer analyzes the reasons for--and/or the consequences of--an action, event, or decision.

Chorus
A group of characters in Greek tragedy (and in later forms of drama), who comment on the action of a play without participation in it.

Chronological Order
A method of organization in which actions or events are presented as they occur (or occurred) in time.

Climactic Order
the organization of ideas from one extreme to another-for example, from least important to most important, from most destructive to least destructive, or from least promising to most promising.

Colloquialism / Colloquial Language
The use of informal words, phrases or even slang in a piece of writing.

Comic Relief
An amusing scene, incident, or speech introduced into serious or tragic elements, as in a play, in order to provide temporary relief from tension, or to intensify the dramatic action.

Descriptive Essay
Descriptive writing says what happened or what another author has discussed; it provides an account of the topic.

Diction
Choice of words, especially with regard to correctness, clearness, or effectiveness. Any of the four generally accepted levels of diction—formal, informal, colloquial, or slang—may be correct in a particular context but incorrect in another or when mixed unintentionally.

Dramatic Irony
A plot device in which the audience's or reader's knowledge of events or individuals surpasses that of the characters. The words and actions of the characters therefore take on a different meaning for the audience or reader than they have for the play's characters. This may happen when, for example, a character reacts in an inappropriate or foolish way or when a character lacks self-awareness and thus acts under false assumptions.

Dramatic Monologue
A literary, usually verse, composition in which a speaker reveals his or her character, often in relation to a critical situation or event, in a monologue addressed to the reader or to a presumed listener.

Elegy
A poem or song composed especially as a lament for a deceased person.

Emotional Appeal
When a writer appeals to an audience's emotions (often through hope, fear, anger or other core emotions) to excite and involve them in the argument, and bring about the desired outcome.

Epic
An extended narrative poem in elevated or dignified language, celebrating the feats of a legendary or traditional hero. Examples include Milton's *Paradise Lost* and Dante's *Inferno*.

Epiphany
A sudden eye-opener regarding the nature of a person or situation. In literary terms, an epiphany is that moment in the story where a character achieves realization, awareness or a feeling of knowledge after which events are seen through the prism of this new light in the story.

Epilogue
A short addition or concluding section at the end of a literary work, often dealing with the future of its characters. Also called afterword.

Epigram
A brief, clever, and memorable statement at the opening of a larger body of work. It often sets what follows into a specific context.

Epitaph
An inscription on a tombstone in memory of the one buried there, and/or A brief literary piece commemorating a deceased person.

Exposition

The portion of a story that introduces important background information to the audience; for example, information about the setting, events occurring before the main plot, characters' back stories, etc.

Extended Metaphor

A metaphor introduced and then further developed throughout all or part of a literary work, especially a poem.

Foil / Character Foil

Another character in a story who contrasts with the main character, usually to highlight one of their attributes.

Formal Essay

The formal essay is preoccupied with ideas, and its treatment is generally serious. The purpose of the formal essayist is to persuade, explain or instruct. Thus, the reader of this essay must pay close attention to the ideas, the way they are presented and the logic of their presentation.

Iambic Pentameter

Iambic pentameter is the name given to a line of verse that consists of five iambs (an iamb being one unstressed syllable followed by one stressed, such as "before").

Indeterminate Ending

Not leading up to a definite result or ending. This can occur if the text's ending does not provide full closure and there are still questions to be answered.

Informal Essay

The informal essay is written mainly for enjoyment. This is not to say that it cannot be informative or persuasive; however, it is less a formal statement than a relaxed expression of opinion, observation, humour or pleasure. A good informal essay has a relaxed style but retains a strong structure, though that structure may be less rigid than in a formal paper.

Irony

A technique of indicating, through either character or plot development, an intention or attitude opposite to that which is actually or implicitly stated; e.g. *The irony of her reply, "How nice!" when I said I had to work all weekend. (See also Dramatic Irony)*

Juxtaposition

A literary device wherein the author places a person, concept, place, idea or theme parallel to another. The purpose of juxtaposing two directly/indirectly related entities close together in literature is to highlight the contrast between the two and compare them.

Lyric

A poem, usually short, that expresses some basic emotion or state of mind. It usually creates a single impression and is highly personal. Sonnets are lyric poems, as is Burns' "A Red, Red Rose."

Metre

A rhythm of accented and unaccented syllables which are organized into patterns, called feet.

Monologue

An extended speech by one person. The term has several closely related meanings. A dramatic monologue is any speech of some duration addressed by a character to a second person. A soliloquy is a type of monologue in which a character directly addresses an audience or speaks his thoughts aloud while alone or while the other actors keep silent.

Objective (language tone etc.)

Something that one's efforts or actions are intended to attain or accomplish; purpose; goal; target. In writing, it's what you hope to achieve.

Ode

A lyric poem of some length, usually of a serious or meditative nature and having an elevated style and formal stanzaic structure.

Oxymoron

A figure of speech in which incongruous or seemingly contradictory terms appear side by side; e.g. "living death" or "paid volunteer."

Paradox

A statement that appears to be self-contradictory or silly but may include a latent truth. It is also used to illustrate an opinion or statement contrary to accepted traditional ideas. A paradox is often used to make a reader think over an idea in innovative way; e.g. "The enemy of my enemy is my friend." Or "Youth is wasted on the young."

Pathos

A quality, as of an experience or a work of art, which arouses feelings of pity, sympathy, tenderness, or sorrow.

Persuasive Essay / Argumentative Essay

Also known as the argumentative essay, it utilizes logic and reason to show that one idea is more legitimate than another idea. It attempts to persuade a reader to adopt a certain point of view or to take a particular action.

Prologue

A preface or introduction to a literary work. In a dramatic work, the term describes a speech, often in verse, addressed to the audience by one or more of the actors at the opening of a play.

Quatrain

A stanza or poem of four lines, usually with alternate rhymes.

Sarcasm

A form of speech where the intended meaning is different from the sentence's or phrase's meaning at face value – usually the opposite; e.g. *"This book clearly took a lot of effort,"* when the meaning implied is that the speaker believes it took no effort at all, or that it required effort, but none was given.

Satire

A literary composition, in verse or prose, in which human folly and vice are held up to scorn, derision, or ridicule. It is often designed to inspire change or reform.

Soliloquy

An utterance or discourse by a person who is talking to himself or herself or is disregardful of or oblivious to any hearers present (often used as a device in drama to disclose a character's innermost thoughts): Hamlet's soliloquy begins with "To be or not to be."

Sonnet

A poem, properly expressive of a single, complete thought, idea, or sentiment, of 14 lines, usually in iambic pentameter, with rhymes arranged according to one of certain definite schemes.

Static Character
A literary or dramatic character who undergoes little or no inner change; a character who does not grow or develop.

Stock / Stereotyped Character
A character type that appears repeatedly in a particular literary genre, one which has certain conventional attributes or attitudes; e.g. The corrupt cop, the town drunk, the noble slave, the prostitute with a heart-of-gold, the emotionless assassin, etc.

Symbol / Symbolism
A literary device that contains several layers of meaning, often concealed at first sight, and is representative of several other aspects/ concepts/ traits than those that are visible in the literal translation alone. Symbol is using an object or action that means something more than its literal meaning;
e.g. The mockingbird, in *To Kill a Mockingbird*, represents innocence, beyond being just a bird species.

Tragedy
A drama or literary work in which the main character is brought to ruin or suffers extreme sorrow, especially as a consequence of a tragic flaw, moral weakness, or inability to cope with unfavourable circumstances.

Understatement
A literary device in which a writer or speaker attributes less importance or conveys less passion than the subject would seem to demand; e.g. "The impending doom of mankind is a matter that should warrant some attention."

Voice

Two definitions: 1) The author's style, the quality that makes his or her writing unique, and which conveys the author's attitude, personality, and character. 2) The characteristic speech and thought patterns of a first-person narrator; a persona. It is one of the most important elements of a piece of writing.

Know the following (and all previous) in Grade 11

Active Voice

When the verb of a sentence is in the active voice, the subject is doing the acting, as in the sentence "Kevin hit the ball." Kevin (the subject of the sentence) acts in relation to the ball. (See also *Passive Voice*).

Antithesis

The direct or exact opposite; e.g. "Give me liberty, or give me death." Or "Hope is the antithesis of despair."

Anecdotal Evidence

Information obtained from personal accounts, examples, and observations. Usually not considered scientifically valid or relevant as proof, but may indicate areas for further investigation and research.

Aphorism

A brief saying, embodying a moral; e.g. Pope's "Some praise at morning what they blame at night / But always think the last opinion right."

Apostrophe

A figure of speech in which an absent person, an abstract concept, or an inanimate object is addressed; e.g. "Moses, hear me." Or "Death, be not proud."

Cacophony

Two definitions: 1) The use of words and phrases that imply strong, harsh sounds within the phrase. These words have jarring and dissonant sounds that create a disturbing, objectionable atmosphere. 2) A harsh, discordant mixture of sounds.

Didactic

Intended to instruct; Morally instructive; Inclined to teach or moralize excessively.

Dissonance

A disruption of harmonic sounds or rhythms. Like cacophony, it refers to a harsh collection of sounds; dissonance is usually intentional, however, and depends more on the organization of sound for a jarring effect, rather than on the unpleasantness of individual words.

Dramatic Form

The specific mode of fiction represented in performance.

Editorial

An article in a publication expressing the opinion of its editors or publishers.

Euphemism

The literary practice of using a comparatively milder or less abrasive form of a negative description instead of its original, unsympathetic form. This device is used when writing about serious matters or "embarrassing" ones. The purpose of euphemisms is to substitute unpleasant and severe words with more genteel ones in order to mask the harshness;
e.g. "Downsizing" instead of "Firing." Or "Friendly fire" instead of "Killed by soldiers on your own side."

Euphony

Agreeableness of sound; pleasing effect to the ear, especially a pleasant sounding or harmonious combination or succession of words. The use of euphony is predominant in literary prose and poetry, where poetic devices such as alliterations, rhymes and assonance are used to create pleasant sounds.

Expert Testimony

A witness who has knowledge not normally possessed by the average person, concerning the topic that he/she is to testify about.

Frame Story

A narrative providing the framework for connecting a series of otherwise unrelated stories, or, a secondary story or stories embedded in the main story.

Interior Monologue

In literature: a form of stream-of-consciousness writing that represents the inner thoughts of a character.

In movies, television: the device of showing a character on screen who does not appear to speak, although the character's voice is heard on the soundtrack to create the illusion that the audience is hearing the character's thoughts.

Literal Language

The primary or strict meaning of the word or words; not figurative or metaphorical.

Octave

A verse form consisting of eight lines of iambic pentameter. The most common rhyme scheme for an octave is *abba abba*.

Parallelism

The use of components in a sentence that are grammatically the same; or similar in their construction, sound, meaning or meter; e.g. "Alice ran into the room, into the garden, and into our hearts."

Parody

Two definitions: 1) A literary or artistic work that imitates the characteristic style of an author or a work for comic effect or ridicule. 2) Something so bad as to be equivalent to intentional mockery; a travesty.

Passive Voice

A verb is in the passive voice when the subject of the sentence is acted on by the verb. For example, in "The ball was thrown by the pitcher," the ball (the subject) receives the action of the verb, and was thrown is in the passive voice. The same sentence cast in the active voice would be, "The pitcher threw the ball." It is usually preferable to use the active voice wherever possible, because it gives a sense of immediacy to the sentence.

Persuasive Technique

The strategy or method that a person or group uses to persuade an audience of something.

Sestet

A poem or stanza containing six lines, especially the last six lines of a Petrarchan sonnet.

Statistical Evidence

A set or collection of numbers that prove a theory or story to be true. Good statistical evidence is very clear about how likely it is to be 'correct'. Data can be delivered with an 80% confidence, or a 95% confidence. In general, the bigger the sample you use, the more likely the answer is to be 'correct'.

Story within a Story
A literary device in which one character within a narrative himself narrates. The inner stories are told either simply to entertain or more usually to act as an example to the other characters. In either case the story often has symbolic and psychological significance for the characters in the outer story. There is often some parallel between the two stories, and the fiction of the inner story is used to reveal the truth in the outer story.

Stream of Consciousness
A literary technique that presents the thoughts and feelings of a character as they occur, or the same from the author himself/herself.

Style
The manner in which an author chooses to write to his or her audience. A style reveals both the writer's personality and voice, but it also shows how she or he perceives the audience. The choice of a conceptual writing style moulds the overall character of the work

Subjective (language tone)
Based on personal thoughts, feelings, experiences, and prejudices. One's own interpretation of facts or events.

Wit
A form of intelligent humour, the ability to say or write things that are clever and usually funny.

Farce
Two definitions: 1) A light, humorous play in which the plot depends upon a skillfully exploited situation rather than upon the development of character. 2) A foolish show; mockery; a ridiculous sham.

Melodrama
A dramatic form characterized by excessive sentiment, exaggerated emotion, sensational and thrilling action, and an artificially-happy ending.

Pastoral
Relating to, or being, a literary or other artistic work that portrays or evokes rural life, usually in an idealized way.

Stylistic Technique
Point of view, tone, diction, narrative pace, humour, imagery, irony, figurative language and many more that give meaning or feel to something written or expressed.

WRITING AND USAGE / GRAMMAR
(OR, HOW TO PREVENT LOSING MARKS
THROUGH EASILY-AVOIDABLE ERROR)

Mechanics include such items as underlining, titles, abbreviations, capitalization, hyphens, numbers, etc. Sometimes punctuation is included under this heading and vice-versa. The number in brackets indicate the grade by which it should be mastered.

Capitalization [8]
The following should be capitalized in all writing:

God and His pronouns

Proper nouns and proper adjectives

First word of a sentence,

First word in a formal statement

First word of a direct quotation

Geographical names

the North, the South
   (but not directions i.e. "Go south on 216th")

Business firms and organizations

Historical events

Calendar items

Nationalities, races and religions

Brand names (but not the item)

Titles of people, books, poems, etc.

Language courses and courses followed by a number

Capitalization Examples:

Mexico **C**ity	a city in Mexico
Glacier **N**ational **P**ark	a national park
Twenty-ninth **S**treet	across the street
Cultus **L**ake	a skier's lake
North **A**merica	northern B.C.
Happy **H**ouse **H**igh **S**chool	a high school
Kwantlen **P**olytechnic **U**niversity	a university in Langley
The **A**merican **R**evolution	a revolution
The **F**ourth of **J**uly	a specific date
English, **F**rench, **M**ath 12	social studies, math.
History 12	a course in history
President Frankr	club president
Toyota **F**orerunner	brand name
Ivory soap	brand name

And then, did she say, "**W**hat is going on?"

Use of Italics [8]

(or **<u>underlining</u>** if you hand write or can't italicize):

Book titles

e.g.   John Steinbeck's *The Pearl* is a classic

Newspapers

e.g.   *The Vancouver Sun* is not right wing at all!

Magazines

e.g.   My favourite magazine is *PC Magazine*

Journals,

e.g.   An informative journal is the *Canadian Journal of Education*

Plays

e.g.   Who could forget *Hamlet* or *Romeo and Juliet*?

Names of ships

e.g.   Have you sailed the good ship *Lollipop*?

Long poems and musical compositions

e.g.   Have you read *Paradise Lost*?

Foreign words or phrases

e.g.   are you part of the *ad hoc* committee?

Use of Quotation Marks [8]
Quotation Marks go around the following:

Articles, Essays,

e.g. you simply must read "Family Planning" in *RP* !

Short Stories,

e.g. "The Sentry" in *Great Short Stories* is superb.

Poems,

e.g. Hopkins's best poem is "God's Grandeur."

Songs,

e.g. I like "Yesterday" by the Beatles.

Chapters of books,

e.g. Chapter 5, "Getting Started" in *Computers* is helpful.

Figures of Speech

e.g. "The Great White Shark" he is.

Using Numbers [8]

Some rules are as follows:

1. Do not begin a sentence with a numeral.

2. Numbers of more than two words should be written in numerals.

3. Hyphenate all compound numbers from twenty-one to ninety-nine.

4. Hyphenate fractions used as adjectives.

5. Write out numbers like second, twenty-fifth, etc., when used ordinarily.

PUNCTUATION

In this section we restrict ourselves again to those areas which seem to be the most problematic in punctuation: quotation marks; semicolon; colon; apostrophe; dash, parentheses.

Semicolon: [9]

1. Use a semicolon between independent clauses not joined by *and, but, or, nor, for , yet.*

e.g.
Take with you only valuable things; leave behind the bulky stuff.

2. Use a semicolon between independent clauses joined by such words as *for example, for instance, besides, moreover, furthermore, therefore, however, instead, hence.*

e.g.
Holiday traffic is often scary; for instance, three people were injured Christmas day.

3. Use a semicolon between items in a series, especially if the items contain commas.

e.g.
The following members are now in the School Board: Bob Smith, Chairman; Darlene Fruggle, vice-chair; Chris Slype, secretary.

Colon: [8]

1 Use a colon to mean "note what follows."

e.g.

Here's what you take along: lotion, volleyball, pop, and a smile.

2. Use a colon when the second of two independent clauses reinforces the first.

e.g.

These seats are the most durable kind: they are reinforced with double stitching.

3. Use a colon for time, Bible texts, volume and page for magazines, and after the salutation of a business letter.

e.g.

4:30 P.M.

John 3:16.

Harper's 198:12.

Dear Mr. Smythe:

Apostrophe: [8]

1. Use an apostrophe to form the possessive of a singular noun.

e.g.   Harry's coat; Ron's opinion; Gus's hat.

NOTE: for nouns of two syllables which end in s it is permissible to add an apostrophe without the s: E.G: Jesus' love;   Julius' girlfriend.

2. For plural noun possession, the apostrophe follows the pluralized noun:

e.g.   girls' gym; Joneses' tennis court;

NOTE: Plural nouns that don't end in s are treated as singular. E.G: Women's room.

3. Personal pronouns *his, hers, its, yours, ours, theirs,* and the relative pronoun *whose* <u>do not</u> require an apostrophe.

e.g.
Is it yours, hers or mine?   This is baseball at its best.
Well, whose book is this?

4. Use an apostrophe and an *s* to form the plural of letters, numbers, abbreviations and signs.

e.g.   Mississippi is spelled with four *s*'s, four *i*'s and two *p*'s.
Instead of a *3* and an *8* he had written two *3*'s
How many *+*'s in this exercise?
If you've seen one UFO, you've seen all the UFO's.

Dash and Parentheses [8/9]

The simplest rule to apply for these "interruptions" in a simple sentence is as follows:

Commas are used to enclose added information in a sentence.

Parentheses are used to enclose directions or clarification in a sentence.

Dashes are used to enclose an abrupt break in thought in a sentence.

Examples:

Allard, who refuses to smoke, is very health conscious.

English students (whom we identified earlier) fare better than Italian students.

The referees--highly paid, no less--should not have gone on strike.

NOTE: Be sure that material within these "interruptions" can be omitted without changing the original meaning or structure of the sentence.

Quotation Marks: [8/9]

1. Commas and periods always go <u>inside</u> the closing quotation marks.

e.g.

I realize that he said "I've seen enough."

"In the meantime," he continued, "I plan to give you a raise."

2. Semicolon and colon always go <u>outside</u> the closing quotation marks.

e.g.

The following can be considered "highbrow reading": Homer, Eliot and Pound.

3. Question marks and exclamation marks go <u>inside</u> if the question is included in the quotation, and <u>outside</u> if the question is part of the larger sentence.

4. If the quotation and the whole sentence both have a question, the question or exclamation mark goes <u>inside</u>. The quoted part takes precedence.

e.g.

"Are the players ready?" asked the referee.

Were you surprised when he said, "Pull over"?

Did you ever ask yourself, "Where will I be in ten years?"

What a pain you are!" she exclaimed.

NOTE: Normally, only one end mark is used at the end of a quotation.

Wrong: Did you ask if Frank said, "I love everything."?
Correct: Did you ask if Frank said, "I love everything"?

5. Use single quotation marks for a quotation within a quotation.

e.g.

Her exact words were, "For tomorrow, read Frost's 'Mending Wall.'"

6. Longer quotations (2 lines or more / 25+ words) are set off from the text, and indented on both sides. Thus there is no need to use quotation marks. Normally, this longer quotation is introduced by a colon. It is wise to use long quotations very sparingly, especially in a short paper.

e.g.

Michelangelo did not paint the Sistine Chapel all in one continuous project. The gap between the two phases influenced the subject and style he used. As Christine Zapella notes:

> In 1510, Michelangelo took a yearlong break from painting the Sistine Chapel. The frescoes painted after this break are characteristically different from the ones he painted before it, and are emblematic of what we think of when we envision the Sistine Chapel paintings. These are the paintings, like *The Creation of Adam*, where the narratives have been paired down to only the essential figures depicted on a monumental scale (45).

71

The Comma: [8/9]

Use a comma to separate two adjectives when the word
and can be inserted between them.
e.g.
He is a strong, healthy man.
We stayed at an expensive summer resort.
> You would not say *expensive and summer resort*, so no
> comma.

Use commas before or surrounding the name or title of a
person directly addressed.
e.g.
Will you, Aisha, do that assignment for me?
Yes, Doctor, I will.
> NOTE: Capitalize a title when directly addressing
> someone.

Use commas to set off expressions that interrupt sentence flow.
e.g.
I am, as you have probably noticed, very nervous about this.

When starting a sentence with a weak clause, use a comma
after it.
e.g.
If you are not sure about this, let me know now.
Wondering where the call had come from, he checked the call
history on the display.

Use a comma after phrases of more than three words that begin
a sentence. If the phrase comes before the true subject of the
sentence, use a comma.
e.g.
To apply for this job, you must have previous experience.
On February 14th, many couples give each other candy or
flowers.

If something or someone is sufficiently identified, the description following it is considered nonessential and should be surrounded by commas.

e.g.

Freddy, who has a limp, was in an accident.

    Freddy is named. The description is non-essential.
    Use a comma.

Use a comma to separate two strong clauses joined by a coordinating conjunction--*and, or, but, for, nor*. You can omit the comma if the clauses are both short.

e.g.

*I have painted the entire house, but he is still working on
    sanding the doors.*
I paint and he writes.

Use a comma to separate a statement from a question.

e.g.

I can go, can't I?

Use a comma to separate contrasting parts of a sentence.

e.g.

That is my money, not yours.
He was badly wounded, but not dead.

Use a comma when beginning sentences with introductory words such as *well*, *now*, or *yes*.

e.g.

Yes, I do need that report.
Well, I never thought I'd live to see the day...

Use commas surrounding words such
as *therefore* and *however* when they are used as interrupters.

e.g.

I would, therefore, like a response.
I would be happy, however, to volunteer for the Red Cross.

TRANSITIONAL WORDS AND PHRASES: [9/10]

Using transitional words and phrases helps papers read more smoothly by providing coherence. **A coherent paper allows the reader** to flow from the first supporting point to the last. **Transitions indicate relations**, whether from sentence to sentence, or from paragraph to paragraph.

Addition:

> also, besides, furthermore, in addition, moreover, again

Consequence:

> accordingly, as a result, consequently, hence, otherwise, so then, therefore, thus, thereupon

Summarizing:

> after all, all in all, all things considered, briefly, by and large, in any case, in any event, in brief, in conclusion, on the whole, in short, in summary, in the final analysis, in the long run, on balance, to sum up, to summarize, finally

Generalizing:

> as a rule, as usual, for the most part, generally, generally speaking, ordinarily, usually, often, frequently, typically

Restatement:

in essence, in other words, namely, that is, that is to say, in short, in brief, to put it differently, therefore

Contrast and Comparison:

in contrast, by the same token, conversely, instead, likewise, on one hand, on the other hand, on the contrary, rather, similarly, yet, but, however, still, nevertheless, in contrast

Sequence:

at first, first of all, to begin with, in the first place, at the same time, for now, for the time being, the next step, in time, in turn, later on, meanwhile, next, then, soon, in the meantime, later, while, earlier, simultaneously, afterward, in conclusion

Illustration:

for example, for instance, for one thing, to illustrate, to demonstrate, as an example, this suggests...

Similarity:

likewise, similar, moreover

Diversion / As an Aside:

by the way, incidentally

THE WRITING PROCESS [10]

Writing Variables

Your consideration of the writing variables will help you to focus your writing and to maintain consistency of style throughout the writing assignment. Applicable to any kind of writing in any subject area, these variables are:

Audience

For whom are you writing? Your teacher, your six-year-old brother or sister, your employer, your student peers, your fellow employees, or your local Member of Parliament? Whatever the case, it will determine your vocabulary, subject content, complexity of sentences, and format. If you want to convince others that your ideas have merit, you have to understand the audience's situation.

Topic

What subject are you writing on? A well written essay has well researched information to back up the claims it makes.

Purpose

Why are you writing? If your answer is simply to get a mark and get the assignment over with, then your paper is going to lack purpose. People write to entertain, to inform, to instruct, to persuade. Decide why you are writing your essay; this will provide a focus for your work.

<u>Persona</u>

What voice are you going to use? Writers sometimes become other people to make their writing become more interesting. Experimenting with other points of view can also increase your understanding of the topic.

<u>Format</u>

What form is your writing going to take? Different forms of writing, such as letters, journals, reports, literary essays, research papers, persuasive essays, and reviews, have specific requirements that must be fulfilled.

KEY WORDS IN WRITING
ASSIGNMENTS AND EXAMS

Some of the more common key words are listed here with a brief explanation.

AGREE OR DISAGREE Support OR contradict a statement; give positive OR negative features; list advantages or disadvantages.

ASSESS Estimate the value of something based on some criteria; give an opinion as to its strong or weak characteristics.

COMMENT ON Give an explanatory note on the main or controversial features of a subject; provide, in addition, a personal opinion on a subject.

COMPARE Give an estimate of the similarity or dissimilarity of one thing to another; give an estimate of the relationship between two things.

CONTRAST Give an estimate of the difference (s) between two things.

CRITICIZE Give an opinion as to the relative merits of a thing, idea, or concept. In criticizing, make a judgment which approves, disapproves, or both.

DEFINE Give the meaning or scope of a word or concept and provide context by establishing its normal limits.

DISCUSS Present points of view on a subject as they might occur in conversation; provide the results of an imaginary examination by debate or argument.

EVALUATE Appraise or assess the value of something based on some known standard; give an opinion as to the advantages or disadvantages involved.

EXPLAIN Give an account of what something is, how it works, or why it is the way it is. Use paraphrasing, provide reasons/examples, or give a step-by-step account.

IDENTIFY Establish clearly the identity of something based on an understood set of considerations; recognize the unique qualities of something and state the criteria used to identify it; simply provide the name of something.

JUSTIFY Give facts, reasons, illustrations, or examples to support a particular, predetermined idea or point of view.

SUMMARIZE Give a brief account of the main points.

EVALUATING SOURCES [10]

In the research process you will encounter many types of resources including books, articles and websites. But not everything you find on your topic will be suitable. How do you make sense of what is out there and evaluate its authority and appropriateness for your research?

SUITABILITY

Scope.
What is the breadth of the article, book, website or other material? Is it a general work that provides an overview of the topic or is it specifically focused on only one aspect of your topic. Does the breadth of the work match your own expectations? Does the resource cover the right time period that you are interested in?

Audience.
Who is the intended audience for this source? Is the material too technical or too clinical? Is it too elementary or basic? You are more likely to retrieve articles written for the appropriate audience if you start off in the right index. For instance, to find resources listing the latest statistics on heart disease you may want to avoid the Medline database which will bring up articles designed for practicing clinicians rather than social science researchers.

Timeliness.
When was the source published? If it is a website, when was it last updated? Avoid using undated websites. Library catalogs and periodical indexes always indicate the publication date in the bibliographic citation.

SCHOLARLY vs POPULAR

A scholarly journal is generally one that is published by and for experts. In order to be published in a scholarly journal, an article must first go through the peer review process in which a group of widely acknowledged experts in a field reviews it for content, scholarly soundness and academic value. Scholarly sources will almost always include:

- Bibliography and footnotes
- Author's name and academic credentials

As a general rule, scholarly journals are not printed on glossy paper, do not contain advertisements for popular consumer items and do not have colorful graphics and illustrations (there are, of course, exceptions).

Popular magazines range from highly respected publications such as Scientific American and The Atlantic Monthly to general interest newsmagazines like Newsweek and US News & World Report. Articles in these publications tend to be written by staff writers or freelance journalists and are geared towards a general audience.

Articles in popular magazines are more likely to be shorter than those in academic journals. While most magazines adhere to editorial standards, articles do not go through a peer review process and rarely contain bibliographic citations.

AUTHORITY

Who is the author? What are his or her academic credentials? What else has this author written? Sometimes information about the author is listed somewhere in the article. Other times, you may need to consult another resource to get background information on them. It helps to search the author's name in a general web search engine like Google.

OTHER INDICATORS

Documentation.
A bibliography, along with footnotes, indicate that the author has consulted other sources and serves to authenticate the information that he or she is presenting. In websites, expect links or footnotes documenting sources, and referring to additional resources and other viewpoints.

Objectivity.
What point of view does the author represent? Is the article an editorial that is trying to argue a position? Is the website sponsored by a company or organization that advocates a certain philosophy? Is the article published in a magazine that has a particular editorial position?

Primary vs. secondary research.
In determining the appropriateness of a resource, it may be helpful to determine whether it is primary research or secondary research.

Primary research presents original research methods or findings for the first time. Examples include:
- A journal article, book, or other publication that presents new findings and new theories, usually with the data
- A newspaper account written by a journalist who was present at the event he or she is describing is a primary source (an eye-witness, first-hand account), and may also be primary "research"

Secondary research does not present new research but rather provides a compilation or evaluation of previously presented material. Examples include:
- A scientific article summarizing research or data, such as in Scientific American, Discover, Annual Review of Genetics, or Biological Reviews

- An encyclopedia entry and entries in most other Reference books
- A textbook

Take an article in a popular magazine such as Mother Jones about the public health aspects of handgun control -- if it relies on interviews with experts and does not present any new research in the area, this article would be considered secondary research.

USING WEBSITES

While most of the strategies listed above for evaluating information can be applied to any type of resource (books, articles or websites), the unfiltered, free-form nature of the Web provides unique challenges in determining a website's appropriateness as an information source. In evaluating a website, these are some questions that you can ask yourself:

- Is there an author of the document? Can you determine the producer's credentials? If you cannot determine the author of the site, then think twice about using it as a resource.
- Is the site sponsored by a group or organization? If it is sponsored by a group or company, does the group advocate a certain philosophy? Try to find and read "About Us" or similar information.
- Is there any bias evident in the site? Is the site trying to sell you a product? Ask why the page was put on the web?
- Is there a date on the website? Is it sufficiently up-to-date? If there is no date, again, think twice about using it. Undated factual or statistical information should never be used.
- How credible and authentic are the links to other resources? Are the links evaluated or annotated in any way?

Manuscript form [8]

You are what you write. In academic writing the marker only sees you through the work you have presented. If your essay or story or report or journal or whatever, is written on torn, dirty paper, or if you produce all sorts of facts to back your statements without citing the source, or if your work is shoddy in any other way, it reflects the time and effort you have put into this work. In short, you have devalued this work. More importantly, it is a reflection of you and your dedication to the task at hand. Hence it is important to not only have the right stuff but also to present it professionally.

The following guidelines are designed for the more formal work; e.g. formal essays, reports, and projects that would normally be typed, though not necessarily so.

Obviously, certain instructors will require somewhat different formats, especially for the less formal assignments; however, for the more formal written output these guidelines should be applicable.

1. **Write on one side of the paper only.**
2. **Double-space the lines of prose.**
3. **Your margins should be 1 inch all the way around.**
4. **The title page should have the title, student's name, subject, instructor's name, school's name, and date.**
5. **Number all pages after title page, preferably at the top right-hand corner.**
6. **Staple together with one staple in the top left-hand corner.**

THE INCAS

past and future

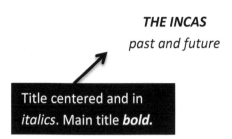

Title centered and in *italics*. Main title **bold**.

by:

Wendy Snarple
89024

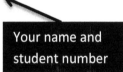

Your name and student number

Teacher, subject, school, and due date

for:

Mr. John Smythe
Social Studies 8
CCHS
Sept. 11, 2014

A NOTE ON TITLE PAGES:

It's time to forget all the things you did in elementary school in regards to title pages. No fancy fonts, no borders, no pictures, and no other embellishments. Keep the title page plain, simple, and according to the model shown here.

Make the font a standard Times Roman, Arial, or Calibri. Keep sizes the same, and only bold the actual title of the essay or assignment.

Do not put into folders, page protectors, or duo tangs, unless specifically instructed to do so.

Assignments submitted online should also have title pages as their first page.

CHOOSING AN APPROPRIATE TITLE:

Your title page's title should reflect the name of your assignment, or the topic of your essay. "Socials project" or "English essay" are **_not_** appropriate titles.

Some good examples would be:

Rewiring the Brain for Creative Potential
the new frontier of neuroscience

Napoleon:
Dictator or Despot?

The Gluten-free Myth

A House Divided
How inconsistent rule use stole the cup
from the Vancouver Canucks

MLA CITATION
IN-TEXT CITATION

In MLA style, referring to the works of others in your text is done by using what is known as **parenthetical citation**. This method involves placing relevant source information in parentheses after a quote or a paraphrase.

General Formatting Rules

- The source information required in a parenthetical citation depends upon the source medium (e.g. Print, Web, DVD) and upon the source's entry on the Works Cited (bibliography) page.
- Any source information that you provide in-text must correspond to the source information on the Works Cited page. Whatever signal word or phrase you provide to your readers in the text, must be the first thing that appears on the left-hand margin of the corresponding entry in the Works Cited List.
- MLA format follows the **author-page** method of in-text citation. This means that the author's last name and the page number(s) from which the quotation or paraphrase is taken must appear in the text, and a complete reference should appear on your Works Cited page.
- The author's name may appear either in the sentence itself or in parentheses following the quotation or paraphrase, but the page number(s) should always appear in the parentheses, not in the text of your sentence.

For example:

Smith states that being completely anonymous "...can free one from all dishwashing duties" (142).

Being completely anonymous "...can free one from all dishwashing duties" (Smith 142).

Smith argued that being completely anonymous could free one from dishwashing duties (142).

The citations in the examples above, (142) and (Smith 142), tell readers that the information in the sentence can be located on page 142 of a work by an author named Smith. If readers want more information about this source, they can turn to the Works Cited page, where, under the name of Smith, they would find the following information:

Smith, John. *The Joys of being Anonymous*. New York: Penguin, 2012. Print.

Formatting Entries

Use the following guide for in-text citations, depending on its source.

Written sources with one author

For Print sources like books, magazines, scholarly journal articles, and newspapers, provide a signal word or phrase (usually the author's last name) and a page number. If you provide the signal word/phrase in the sentence, you do not need to include it in the parenthetical citation. Examples, again:

Being completely anonymous "...can free one from all dishwashing duties" (Smith 142).

Smith argued that being completely anonymous could free one from dishwashing duties (142).

Written sources with two or more authors

For a source with **three or fewer authors**, list the authors' last names in the text or in the parenthetical citation:

Smith, Doe, and Smyth argue that being anonymous is the greatest joy a person can attain (34).

The authors state, "Being anonymous is truly the greatest joy a person or pet can attain" (Smith, Doe, and Smyth 34).

For a source with **more than three authors**, use the work's bibliographic information as a guide for your citation. Provide the first author's last name followed by et al. or list all the last names.

Slenderman et al. argue against Smith, Doe, and Smyth's claim. They state that being known is a far greater joy (54).

Other experts on the subject argue that Smith, Doe, and Smyth fail to truly understand human need (Slenderman et al. 54).

Or... if you wish to list them all:

Slenderman, Sedwick, Jones, Mulkivin, and Groot argue against Smith, Doe, and Smyth's claim. They state that being known is a far greater joy (54).

Two or more written sources by the same author

If you cite more than one work by a particular author, include a shortened title for the particular work from which you are quoting to distinguish it from the others. Put short titles of books in italics and short titles of articles in quotation marks.

Citing two articles by the same author:

Smith argues that being anonymous allows one to avoid painful jury duty ("Fading slowly" 38), although he does acknowledge that being invisible without bringing your pets along does cause them to starve to death more readily ("Anonymizing your Pets" 17).

Citing two books by the same author:

Smith argues that being anonymous allows one to avoid painful jury duty (*The Joys of being Anonymous* 78), although he does acknowledge that being invisible without bringing your pets along does cause them to starve to death more readily (*Blending in Entirely* 17).

Two Authors with the same last name

Sometimes more information is necessary to identify the source from which a quotation is taken. For instance, if two or more authors have the same last name, provide both authors' first initials (or even the authors' full name if different authors share initials) in your citation. For example:

Some men love being invisible (J. Smith 22), while others seem to hate it (A. Smith 16).

Sources with a Corporate Author / No known Author

When a source has a corporate author, it is acceptable to use the name of the corporation followed by the page number for the in-text citation. You should also use abbreviations (e.g., nat'l for national) where appropriate.

When a source has no known author, use a shortened title of the work instead of an author name. Place the title in quotation marks if it's a short work (such as an article) or italicize it if it's a longer work (e.g. plays, books, television shows, entire Web sites) and provide a page number.

Example:

In a government pamphlet for the invisible, several warnings are given against pursuing the concept of full anonymity ("Dangers of Fading from Society" 3).

Translated Source

Cite a translated book just as you would a normal book with an author. Do not list the translator with your in text citation, but only in the Works Cited.

Source / Book with a different Edition

Cite the book the same as you would another book, depending on number of authors. Use the edition information only in your Works Cited page.

Source with an Author and an Editor

Cite the book as would any other, including the author information in text, and the author plus editor information on the Works Cited page.

Source with just an Editor, and no Author

When no author is listed, use the editor in your in text citation, and follow the format for Works Cited that follows this pattern.

Essay or Articles / Poems or Short Stories

All of the above-mentioned sources use the same pattern as other written works, depending on author(s) or editor(s). Be sure that these works are done in quotation marks, and are not put into italics.

One poet screams his frustration at constantly being noticed by his landlady, "How can you see me? / Do I not blend? / Is my hope at fading / ever at an end?" ("Now you don't" Jones 12).

Dictionary or Encyclopedia Entry

Most dictionaries and encyclopedias will not have a named author. Your Works Cited entry will be listed according to the entry or article title, and so you do the same thing here.

The word *anonymous* has a surprisingly complex etymology ("Anonymous").

A book's Introduction, Foreword, Afterword, or Preface

Cite material from this portion of a book the same was as any other portion. In your Works Cited, you'll indicate that this is not part of the main body text.

The Bible, or other Religious Text

In your parenthetical citation, give the book, chapter, and verse (or their equivalent), separated by periods. Common abbreviations for books of the Bible are acceptable. For the first citation, list also the translation or version that you are using.

Consider the words of Solomon: "If your enemy is hungry, give him bread to eat; and if he is thirsty, give him water to drink" (*Oxford Annotated Bible*, Prov. 25.21).

The wise men from the east are often referred to as "magi," indicating they used divination (Matt. 2:1).

Allah is introduced to the faithful as "The Entirely Merciful, the Especially Merciful" (Qu'ran 1:1).

Pamphlet or Brochure with no indicated Author

Use the procedure outlined for a source with a corporate author or no known author. Refer to the Works Cited section for specifics relating to this format.

Dissertation or Thesis

For a dissertation or thesis, cite it in text in the same format you would for an article by a single author. The Works Cited portion will specifically indicate that it is a published or unpublished dissertation or thesis.

Magazine Article / Newspaper Article

Cite these sources in text the same way as you would for any other source with an author. The Works Cited page will differentiate between types of sources. When putting in the page number, be aware of the non-standard page numbering system used in many papers.
If there is no listed author, than follow that format (using article name) instead.

```
One  reporter  attempted  to  interview  an  anonymous
community  member,  but  was  unable  to  find  him
(Frankerzwing A2).
```

Or...

```
One  reporter  attempted  to  interview  an  anonymous
community  member,  but  was  unable  to  find  him
("Failing to find the Anonymous" A2).
```

Editorial or Letter to the Editor

Use the procedure for any other article, using the author's name if it is provided, and the title or heading of the editorial or letter, if it is not provided.

Article without an Author

Cite the article in text with the article name, referencing its page number as normal. The Works Cited page will list the entry by article title as well.

Article in a Scholarly Journal

Cite articles from journals the same way as any other work with an author (if provided) or without (if not provided). Page numbering may be different, so be sure to match the original in that regard.

Website

Cite a website page, article, or section in the same way as you would cite an article. Provide author if it is provided, and use the article or section title if it is not. Page numbers are not used for web sources, so that is not required.

One website suggested that being anonymous is as simple as covering oneself with invisible ink ("Looking to vanish forever? You Can!").

Online-Only Journal / Printed and Online Journal

Both these sources are cited in text as any other work with a provided author. For online-only sources, no page number is used, unless it is specifically broken down that way. Printed journals will include page numbers, and their online versions will as well.

Online Database

Cite articles from an online database the same as any other source with an author. The only difference comes in the Works Cited entry, which must include the name of the database service as part of its entry.

E-mail message content

Cite E-mail messages in text by the author's name. If there are several different E-mail messages being cited, add the subject heading of the email to the citation.

In an E-mail message, he stated that he had managed to disconnect from the real world, but remained an active participant in the virtual world (Smith).

Or..

In one E-mail, he stated he hated life ("Life Sucks" Smith). However, he later wrote that he wanted to live forever ("Life is Awesome again!" Smith).

Listserv / Blog / Reddit / Tweet / Facebook Sources

Use the format above for E-mail sources in relation to these sources as well. Use the author's name when possible, and the name of the posting when it is not provided. For Tweets, the user name can replace the author name as needed, but one of the two is always available. See the Works Cited section for more information.

Film source in Theatre / Out on DVD or Blu-ray

Cite an electronic performance work in the same way you would cite a book. Add emphasis on actor or director in the Works Cited section. Put the title in italics for a movie title or show title, and use quotes for episode titles in a show's series.

Radio and Television Programs

For radio programs, cite the same way you would an article. For television programs, use the article format for a specific episode, and the book format if you are citing the entire show.

Music and Sound Recordings

Use the same citation format as you would for a book or article by an author. Use the artist's name alone if you are citing only one composition by that artist. If you are quoting several, indicate the name of the recording track, album, or program in your citation.

MLA CITATION
WORKS CITED PAGE

General Formatting

- Begin your Works Cited page on a separate page from the rest of your assignment. It should have the same margins and spacing as the rest of your paper.
- Put the words **Works Cited** at the top of the page, centered, and not in italics or underlined.
- Double-space all entries, but do not add an extra space between one entry and another.
- Indent the second and following lines of each entry by 0.5 inches (1.27 cm), using a *hanging indent*.
- If citing multiple different works by the same author, you only list his/her name once. Following entries go below the first, and use three dashes in place of his/her name.

    ---, etc...   (*see examples following*)

New Rules for MLA

- Due to the increase in digital and Internet sources, students must now indicate the method of publication with all entries (ie: Print, DVD, CD, CD-ROM, Blu-ray, Web, Kindle file, EPUB file, Nook file, MP3, Digital file).
- You are no longer required to provide full web links for online sources, unless your instructor requests it.
- Websites listed should not have the www or http:// as part of their citation.

    (ie: *CNN.com* and **not** http://*www.CNN.com*)
- If you are citing an item that was originally published in print, but was retrieved from an online database, you must name the database in italics (ie: *EBSCO*).

Formatting Entries

A source follows the standard MLA style of last name, first name format. The basic form for a book citation is:

```
Lastname, Firstname. Title of Book. City of
     Publication: Publisher, Year of Publication.
     Medium of Publication.
```

The use of punctuation, and the use of italics, is essential for accuracy. Examples given here will show the correct formatting. Be sure to follow it precisely. Only the book title is in *italics*.

Books with one author

```
Smith, John. The Joys of being Anonymous. New York:
     Penguin, 2012. Print.
```

Books with two (or more) authors

For two authors, the first given name is put in the last name, first name format. The second name is put normally, with first name followed by last name.

```
Smith, John, and Jane Doe. The Shared Joys of being
     Anonymous. New York: Penguin, 2013. Print.
```

If there are more than three authors, you list only the first author followed by the phrase et al. (Latin for "and others") in place of the subsequent authors' names.

```
Smith, John, et al. The Continued Shared Joys of
     being Anonymous. New York: Penguin, 2014.
     Kindle File.
```

Two or more books by the same author

List the author's works in alphabetical order, by title. Ignore articles like *A*, *An*, and *The*, when sorting. Use the formatting above for the first entry only, and then use three hyphens and a period in subsequent entries.

Smith, John. *The Joys of being Anonymous*. New York: Penguin, 2012. Print.

---. *Continuing to Fade from View*. New York: Nelson Publishing, 2012. Print.

Books by an Organization or Corporation

A book may be published by a committee, commission, or a group that does not list its individual members on the title page. List the name of the corporation or group where the author's name usually goes. Ignore A, An, and The, and put after the group's name (if included).

Anonymous Association, The. *The Joys of being Anonymous Together*. New York: Random House, 2014. Print.

Books with no known author

In rare instances, neither the author, nor the organization, are identified. In this case, list by title of the book according to your alphabetical list. In the example below, the book would go between *Adams, Susan* and *Berkotz, Frank.*

Anonymous is Awesome. Boston: Penguin, 2014. Print.

Books that have been Translated

Cite these as you would any other book, but add "Trans." and the names of the translators. Translator names are done in the first name, last name format.

Szwrkzy, Olguff. *Madness in Anonymity: Going Crazy.*
    Trans. Joe Smith and Jane Doe. New York:
    Random House, 1988. EPUB File.

An Edition of a Book

Sometimes books, especially reference ones, will have more than one edition. In this case, add the number of the edition (along with ed.) after the title.

Smith, John. *The Joys of being Anonymous.* 2nd ed. New
    York: Penguin, 2013. Print.

A Book with an Author and an Editor

A book may be re-published after an author's death, and given editing or reformatting. In other cases, the editor adds material alongside an author. List the author first, as per usual listings, and add the editor similar to how you add a translator. In this case, "Ed." indicates a single editor, and "Eds." indicates one or more (see both examples below).

Smith, John. *The Joys of being Anonymous.* Ed. Mary
    Smyth. New York: Penguin, 2013. Print.

Smith, John. *The Joys of being Anonymous.* Eds. Mary
    Smyth and James Doe. New York: Penguin, 2013.
    Print.

A Book with an Editor, but no listed Author

With no listed author, use the editor's name in its place, but use the "Ed." behind it.

Smyth, Mary. Ed. *The Joys of being Anonymous.* New York: Penguin, 2013. Print.

A Work in an Anthology, Reference, or Collection

Works may include an **essay** in a collection, or an **article** in a magazine. The basic form for this sort of citation is as follows:

Last name, First name. "Title of Essay." *Title of Collection.* Ed. Editor's Name(s). City of Publication: Publisher, Year. Page range of entry. Medium of Publication.

Note that the order is somewhat different. For example, the "Ed." comes before the editor's name, instead of after it. There is also a page range now, so a reader could find that specific article back again. If the source is electronic, such as a Kindle book, page numbers do not remain static, but alter according to font and screen size. In those instances, leave out the page range.

Smith, Joe. "Making yourself vanish." *A Guide for Disappearance.* Ed. Mary Smyth. New York: Smoke Publications, 2002. 29-39. Print.

Smith, Joe. "Making yourself vanish." *A Guide for Disappearance.* Ed. Mary Smyth. New York: Smoke Publications, 2002. Kindle File.

For a **poem** or a **short story**, it follows the same basic format:

```
Smith, Joe. "Ever Fading." 100 Forgotten Poems. Ed.
    Mary Smyth. New York: Penguin, 2012. 56. Print.

Doe, Jane. "Invisible Girl." The Book of Great
    Canadian Writers of Obscurity. Ed. Joe Smith. New
    York: Vintage Publishing, 1999. EPUB File.
```

If the collection is all from the same author, then there may be no editor to reference.

```
Smith, Joe. "Still Fading." Selected Silly Poems. New
    York: Penguin, 2014. 106-110. Print.
```

Article in Reference Book – Dictionaries and Encyclopedias

Cite the reference like you would any other, but do not include the publisher information. If the book is organized alphabetically, do not list the volume or page number.

```
"Invisibility." The Oxford Dictionary. 2nd ed. 2007.
    Print.
```

A book's Introduction, Foreword, Afterword, or Preface

Write the name of the author(s) of the reference you are citing, and give the name of the portion being cited. Do not use italics or quotations for that portion, but italicize the book title as normal. If portion cited and book author are different, put full author's name in. ("By Smith." Becomes "By Sam Jones.")

```
Smith, James. Introduction. Blending in Entirely. By
    Smith. New York: Penguin, 2013. 1-6. Print.
```

106

The Bible, or other Religious Text

Give the name of the specific edition you are using, any editor(s) associated with it, followed by the publication information.

The New International Study Bible. Ed. Susan Jones. New York: Zondervan Publishing, 1986. Print.

The Holy Qu'ran. Ed. Mohammad Surari. New York: Halal Publishing, 2001. Print.

Pamphlets and Brochures

Most small printings of this nature will not have an author, or even a corporate publisher listed. If it does, cite as per a book with a corporate author. Otherwise, list title and originating organization for the information provided.

Effective Composting. Langley: Organic Growers and Fertilizers, 2003. Print.

Dissertations and Thesis

Dissertations and master's theses may be used as sources whether they are officially published or not. Cite the work as you would a book, but include the designation Diss. (or MA/MS thesis) followed by the degree-granting school and the year the degree was awarded.

If the dissertation is published, put the title in italics:

Smith, John. *Finding the Lost and Invisible*. Diss. Simon Fraser University, 2002. Print.

If the dissertation is not published, put the title in quotation marks:

```
Smith, John. "Finding the Lost and Invisible." MA
     thesis. Simon Fraser University, 2002. Print.
```

Magazine Article

List the author, putting the title of the article in quotation marks, and the magazine title in italics. Follow that with the date of publication, abbreviating the month. The format is:

```
Author(s). "Title of Article." Title of
     Periodical Day Month Year: pages. Medium of
     publication.
```

For Example:

```
Doe, Jane. "I feel so alone." Cosmopolitan 15 June.
     2009: 14-48. Print.
```

Article in a Newspaper

Cite a newspaper article as you would a magazine, but note the different page numbering in newspapers. If there is more than one edition available for that date (as in an early and late edition), identify the edition following the date.

```
Smith, John. "Fear of Vanishing." The Globe and
     Mail 14 May 2013 early ed.: A6. Print.
```

Editorial or Letter to the Editor

Cite as you would any article in a periodical, but include the designators "Editorial" or "Letter" to identify the type of work it is.

"Ghosts and Men." Editorial. *The Province.* ed. 31
        Oct. 2013: C12. Print.

Doe, Jane. Letter. *Washington Post.* 12 Mar. 2012:
        B17. Print.

Articles without a defined author

Cite the article title first, and then finish the citation as you would any other for that kind of periodical.

"Being Invisible in Business and Investing." *The
        Economist* 16 May 2012: 22. Print.

Articles in a Scholarly Journal

These citations are the same as those for Magazines, but will require issue numbers, normally in the volume.issue format, followed the publication year in brackets.

Author(s). "Title of Article." *Title of
        Journal* Volume.Issue (Year): pages. Medium of
        publication.

Becomes...

Smith, John. "Disappearing Pets." *Biomechanics
        Journal* 12.4 (2002): 11-20. Print.

Citing a Web Site

It is necessary to list your date of access because web pages are often updated, and information available on one date may no longer be available later. If a URL is required or you chose to include one, be sure to include the complete address for the site. (Note: The first examples do not include a URL because MLA no longer requires a URL to be included.)

Remember to use *n.p.* if no publisher name is available and *n.d.* if no publishing date is given… and often it isn't.

The basic format is as follows:

```
Editor, author, or compiler name (if
        available). "Page or article title." Name of
        Site. Version number. Name of
        institution/organization affiliated with the
        site (sponsor or publisher), date of resource
        creation (if available). Medium of
        publication. Date of access.
```

Example (with relevant information provided on the web page):

```
Smith, John. "Be completely unnoticed." eHow. Demand
        Media, 10 Jan. 2000. Web. 14 Feb. 2011.
```

Example (with relevant information missing on the web page):

```
"Be completely unnoticed." eHow. n.p., n.d. Web. 14
        Feb. 2011.
```

Or… With Link:

```
"Be completely unnoticed." eHow. n.p., n.d. Web. 14
        Feb. 2011. <eHow.com/articles/13534.html>.
```

Article in an Online Scholarly Journal

For all online scholarly journals, provide the author(s) name(s), the name of the article in quotation marks, the title of the publication in italics, all volume and issue numbers, and the year of publication.

Article in an Online-only Scholarly Journal

MLA requires a page range for articles that appear in Scholarly Journals. If the journal you are citing appears exclusively in an online format and does not make use of page numbers, use the abbreviation *n. pag.* to denote that there are no page numbers available for the publication.

Doe, Jane. "Fading Kids: The Invisible Youth." *Social Work and Youth: The Upstart Online Journal* 1.3 (2012): n. pag. Web. 10 Feb 2013.

Online Scholarly Journal that also appears in Print

Cite articles in online scholarly journals that also appear in print as you would a scholarly journal in print, including the page range of the article. Provide the medium of publication that you used (in this case, *Web*) and the date of access.

Doe, Jane. "Fading Kids: The Invisible Youth." *Social Work and Youth: The Upstart Journal* 1.3 (2012): 223-234. Web. 10 Feb 2013.

Article from an Online Database

The format here is exactly the same as the one above, but add in the database service used (in the example below, *EBSCO*). If the web link is required, it can be added as well. Both examples are provided.

Doe, Jane. "Fading Kids: The Invisible Youth." *Social Work and Youth: The Upstart Journal* 1.3 (2012): 223-234. *EBSCO*. Web. 10 Feb 2013.

Or...with the link:

Doe, Jane. "Fading Kids: The Invisible Youth." *Social Work and Youth: The Upstart Journal* 1.3 (2012): 223-234. *EBSCO*. Web. 10 Feb 2013. <ebscohost.com/articles/journals/4356LD.html>.

E-mail Messages or E-mail Interviews

State the author of the message, the subject line in quotation marks, the message recipient, the date the message was sent, and the medium of publication (in this case, always E-mail).

Doe, Jane. "Re: Can cats turn transparent?" Message to Joe Smith. 21 Dec. 2001. E-mail.

If the message was sent to the author of the paper, put that in instead:

Doe, Jane. "Re: Can cats turn transparent?" Message to the author. 21 Dec. 2001. E-mail.

Listserv, Discussion Group, Blog Posting, Reddit, FaceBook

Cite Web postings as you would a standard Web Site entry. Provide the author of the work, the title of the posting in quotation marks, the Web site name in italics, the publisher, and the posting date. Follow with the medium of publication and the date of access.

Include screen names as author names when author name is not known or given. If both names are known, place the author's name in brackets. Remember if the publisher of the site is unknown, use the abbreviation *n.p.*

Editor, screen name, author, or compiler name (if available). "Posting Title." *Name of Site.* Version number (if available). Name of institution/organization affiliated with the site (sponsor or publisher). Medium of publication. Date of access.

For Example:

BoardFreek22 [Joe Smith]. "Re: Best Strategy: Crops or Kids in Agricola?" *BoardGameGeek.* BoardGameGeek, 19 Oct. 2012. Web. 5 Apr. 2013.

Or… with less information available:

BoardFreek22. "Re: Best Strategy: Crops or Kids in Agricola?" *BoardGameGeek.* *n.p.* Web. 5 Apr. 2013.

A Tweet

Begin with the user's name (Last Name, First Name if known) followed by his/her Twitter username in parentheses, and a period. Place the tweet in its entirety in quotations, inserting a period after. Include the date and time of posting, using the reader's time zone. Separate the date and time with a comma and end with a period. Include the word "Tweet" afterwards as the medium of access.

For Example:

```
Uber Facts (UberFacts). "There are an estimated 35-
     50 active serial killers in the United
     States." 24 Feb. 2014, 8:46 p.m. Tweet.
```

Work of Art – Painting, Sculpture, Photograph

Include the artist's name. Give the title of the artwork in italics. Provide the date of composition. If the date of composition is unknown, place the abbreviation *n.d.* in place of the date. Follow this by the information for the source in which the photograph appears, including page or reference numbers, as per book sources.

```
Buonarroti, Michelangelo. Moses. 1513. Art Through
     the Ages. 10th ed. By Joe Smith and Mary
     Smyth. Rome: Vatican Press. 39. Print.
```

Films and Movies – In Theatre / On DVD or Blu-ray

List films (in **theaters** or not yet on DVD or video) by their title. Include the name of the director, the film studio or distributor, and the release year. If relevant, list performer names after the director's name. Use the abbreviation perf. to head the list. List film as the medium of publication.

Example:

The Usual Suspects. Dir. Bryan Singer. Perf. Kevin
Spacey, Gabriel Byrne, Chazz Palminteri,
Stephen Baldwin, and Benecio del Toro.
Polygram, 1995. Film.

To emphasize specific performers (*perf*.) or directors (*dir*.), begin the citation with the name of the desired performer or director, followed by the appropriate abbreviation.

Lucas, George, dir. *Star Wars Episode IV: A New Hope*.
Twentieth Century Fox, 1977. Film.

For films released on **DVD** or **Blu-ray**, replace the date with the year it was released on that format, and replace the medium of the item with the appropriate one:

Lucas, George, dir. *Star Wars Episode IV: A New Hope
- Extended Edition*. Twentieth Century Fox,
2012. Blu-ray.

Television or Radio Programs

Begin with the title of the episode in quotation marks. Provide the name of the series or program in italics. Also include the network name, call letters of the station followed by the city, and the date of broadcast. End with the publication medium (e.g. *Television, Radio*).

Example:

"Darkness Falls." *The X-Files*. Fox. WXIA, Atlanta. 15
    Apr. 1994. Television.

For television episodes on DVD or Blu-ray, cite like films. Begin with the episode name in quotation marks, followed by the series name in italics. When the title of the collection of recordings is different than the original series (e.g., the show Friends is in DVD release under the title *Friends: The Complete Sixth Season*), list the title that would help locate the recording. Give the distributor name followed by the date of distribution. End with the medium of publication (e.g. *DVD, Blu-ray*).

You may choose to include information about directors, writers, performers, producers between the title and the distributor name. Use appropriate abbreviations for these contributors (e.g. *dir., writ., perf., prod.*).

"The One Where Chandler Can't Cry." *Friends: The
    Complete Sixth Season*. Writ. Andrew Reich and
    Ted Cohen. Dir. Kevin Bright. Warner Brothers,
    2004. Blu-ray.

Music and Sound Recordings

List sound recordings in such a way that they can easily be found by readers. Citations begin with the artist name or by composers (*comp.*) or performers (*perf.*). Otherwise, list composer and performer information after the album title.

Use the appropriate abbreviation after the person's name and a comma, when needed. Put individual song titles in quotation marks. Album names are italicized like books are. Provide the name of the recording manufacturer followed by the publication date (or *n.d.*, if date is unknown).

Example – Full Albums:

The Killers. *Battleborn*. Blackbird Studio, 2012. CD.

Example – Single Song / Audio Track:

Editors. "Bricks and Mortar." *In This Light and On This Evening*. Kitchenware Records, 2009. MP3.

CHICAGO STYLE CITATION
FOOTNOTE & ENDNOTE CITATION
BIBLIOGRAPHICAL ENTRIES

In Chicago style, writers use the **NB system** (notes/bibliography) to provide both citation information, and to grant the ability to comment or expand on materials used as sources. It is most commonly used in History or Law courses, and helps keep body text neat and uncluttered, especially when many sources are used.

General Formatting Rules

- A superscript number (e.g. ^{12}) corresponding to a source quoted or used, is provided along with full bibliographic information, and placed at the bottom of the page where it is used (footnote) or on a page at the end of the document (endnote).
- The first note for each source should include *all* relevant information about the source: author's full name, source title, and facts of publication. If you cite the same source again, the note need only include the surname of the author, a shortened form of the title (if more than four words), and page number(s).
- If you cite the same source and page number(s) from a single source two or more times consecutively, the corresponding note should use the word "Ibid.," an abbreviated form of the Latin *ibidem*, which means "in the same place." If you use the same source but a different page number, the corresponding note should use "Ibid." followed by a comma and the new page number(s). (see Ibid. example following)

Use of Ibid. / Subsequent References

First Reference:

> [1] John Smith, *The Joys of being Anonymous.* (New York: Penguin, 2012), 123.

Following Reference (following immediately after first):

> [2] Ibid., 212.

If a third reference follows, not from John Smith, then it follows the pattern of the first, above.

A later reference to Smith's book would then use the following format, putting in the author's name, and the page number. If there are two sources by Smith, then use the title (shortened).

> [4] Smith, 225.

> [4] Smith, *The Joys of being Anonymous.* 225.

Rules for Bibliographies

In the NB system, the bibliography provides an alphabetical list of all sources used in a given work. This page, titled **Bibliography**, is placed at the end of the work. It should include all sources cited within the work and may sometimes include other relevant sources that were not cited but provide further reading.

Although bibliographic entries for various sources may be formatted differently, all included sources (books, articles, Web sites, etc.) are arranged alphabetically by author's last name. If no author or editor is listed, the title or keyword by which the reader would search for the source may be used instead.

Common Elements

All entries in the bibliography will include the author (or editor, compiler, translator), title, and publication information.

Author's Names

The author's name is inverted in the bibliography, placing the last name first and separating the last name and first name with a comma; for example, John Smith becomes Smith, John. (If an author is not listed first, this applies to compilers, translators, etc.)

Titles

Titles of books and journals are italicized. Titles of articles, chapters, poems, etc. are placed in quotation marks.

Publication Information

The year of publication is listed after the publisher or journal name.

Punctuation

In a bibliography, all major elements are separated by periods.

Formatting Entries

Use the following guide for footnote/endnote citations and bibliographic entries, depending on its source. Both will be listed for each entry here.

General rules for entries:

Footnote:

[1] Firstname Lastname, *Title of Book* (Place of publication: Publisher, Year of publication), page number(s).

Bibliography:
Use the "Hanging Indent" and double-spacing for entries. Do not apply additional spacing between entries, however.

Lastname, Firstname. *Title of Book*. Place of publication: Publisher, Year of publication.

Written sources with one author

Footnote:

[1] John Smith, *The Joys of Being Anonymous* (New York: Penguin, 2012), 71.

Bibliography:

Smith, John. *The Joys of Being Anonymous*. New York: Penguin, 2012.

Written sources with two authors

Note that in the bibliographical entry, the second author's name is given in a first name, last name format.

<u>Footnote:</u>

[2] John Smith and Jane Doe, *Being a Part of the Wallpaper* (London: King's Press, 2004), 241-251.

<u>Bibliography:</u>

Smith, John, and Jane Doe. *Being a Part of the Wallpaper*. London: King's Press, 2004.

Written sources with three or more authors

If there are more than two authors, you list only the first author followed by the phrase et al. (Latin for "and others") in place of the subsequent authors' names.

<u>Footnote:</u>

[2] John Smith, et al., *Fading into the Mattress Coils*. (Boston: Rockstone Printing, 2012), 41-51.

<u>Bibliography:</u>

Smith, John, et al. *Fading into the Mattress Coils*. Boston: Rockstone Printing, 2012.

Two or more written sources by the same author

<u>Footnote:</u>

Make each entry as per the guidelines laid out here, only using Ibid. when citing from the same source twice (or more) in a row.

<u>Bibliography:</u>

List the author's works in alphabetical order, by title. Ignore articles like *A*, *An*, and *The*, when sorting. Use the formatting above for the first entry only, and then use three hyphens and a period in subsequent entries.

Smith, John. *The Joys of Being Anonymous*. New York: Penguin, 2012.

---. *Continuing to Fade from View*. New York: Nelson Publishing, 2013.

Two Authors with the same last name

Cite normally for footnote entries. Put bibliography entries in alphabetical order, according to last name, and then first name.

Smith, John, et al. *Fading into the Mattress Coils*. Boston: Rockstone Printing, 2012.

Smith, Zeke. *Mattress Coils are for Sissies*. New York: Penguin, 2013.

Sources with a Corporate Author / No known Author

If the author of the work is unknown, and there is no listed editor, use just the title of the source as its citation. Ignore A, An, or The when determining its alphabetical placement, but keep as part of the title.

<u>Footnote:</u>

⁵ *The Atlas of Places to Vanish* (New York: Barnes, 2001), 88.

<u>Bibliography:</u>

The Atlas of Places to Vanish. New York: Barnes, 2001

Translated Source

For translated sources, follow the standard format, but add "trans." to the footnote. Then then the name of the translator in a first name, last name format. Publisher and other information follows normally.
In the bibliography, use "Translated by" instead of the abbreviation.

<u>Footnote:</u>

³ Fredrico Cortez, *Transparency*, trans. Joe Smyth (New York: Pantheon Books, 2000), 65.

<u>Bibliography:</u>

Cortez, Fredrico. *Transparency*. Translated by Joe Smyth. New York: Pantheon Books, 2000.

Source / Book with a different Edition

If the edition you are using is not the first edition, then include the edition number in your citation. It comes after the title, and uses the abbreviation "ed." in both the footnote and the bibliography.

Footnote:

⁹ Jane Doe, *Whither goes my Goldfish?,* 4th ed. (New York: Fatfish Press, 2002), 6.

Bibliography:

Doe, Jane. *Whither goes my Goldfish?,* 4th ed. New York: Fatfish Press, 2002.

Source with an Author and an Editor

Use the same basic format as for a translated work, using "ed." for the footnote entry, and the longer "Edited by" for the bibliography. *Note: This differs from a source with an editor and no stated author.*

Footnote:

⁴ Samuel Doe, *Researches into Fading Families,* ed. Frank Bermaan (New York: Penguin, 2012), 94.

Bibliography:

Doe, Samuel. *Researches into Fading Families,* Edited by Frank Bermaan. New York: Penguin, 2012.

Source with just an Editor, and no Author

Cite a work with an editor, and no stated author, the same way as a source with just an author. Simply add "ed." After the name of the editor. If there is a compiler listed instead, use "comp." *Note: This differs from a source with both a named author and an editor.*

Footnote:

¹² Billy Glass, ed. *Songs to People I have Lost* (Chicago: Blackhawk Press, 2013), 22.

Bibliography:

Glass, Billy., ed. *Songs to People I have Lost.* Chicago: Blackhawk Press, 2013.

Essay or Articles / Poems or Short Stories

For any source that is part of a larger work not fully written by your cited author, put the cited section in quotation marks, and the overall source in italics. Use "in" to note that your source is within another broader collection.

Footnote:

¹¹ Joe Smith, "Invisible Spouses," in *Anonymous Actions*, ed. John Doe et al. (Chicago: University of Chicago Press, 2011), 72.

Bibliography:

Smith, Joe. "Invisible Spouses," in *Anonymous Actions*, ed. John Doe et al. Chicago: University of Chicago Press, 2011.

Dictionary or Encyclopedia Entry

Citations from well-known books, such as a dictionary or encyclopedia can be listed with "s. v." (This is Latin for *sub verbo*, "under the word."). Reference works that are less familiar should follow the normal style for a reference book with author(s) and/or editor(s).

Footnote:

[12] *Encyclopedia Britannica*, 12th ed., s.v. "Invisible."

Bibliography:

"Invisible." In *Encyclopedia Britannica*, 12th ed. Edited by Solomon Grundy. New York: Penguin, 2002.

A book's Introduction, Foreword, Afterword, or Preface

When citing an introduction, foreword, afterword, or preface, use the appropriate phrase to denote where it comes from, and apply whatever page numbering scheme it may have.

Footnote:

[7] James Rieger, introduction to *Frankenstein*, by Mary Wollstonecraft Shelley (Chicago: University of Chicago Press, 1982), xx-xxi.

Bibliography:

Rieger, James. Introduction to *Frankenstein*, by Mary Wollstonecraft Shelley, xi-xxxvii. Chicago: University of Chicago Press, 1982.

The Bible, or other Religious Text

The Bible is handled differently from other works, in that you do not need to cite it in your bibliography, but do need its footnote citation. The same goes for books like the Qu'ran. If you are citing non-scripture passages, such as introduction notes, then you cite it as per instructions for Introductions, Forewords, Afterwords, or Prefaces.

In the footnote, include the full or abbreviated name of the book, the chapter and verse, and the translation used. The Qu'ran has names for its sections, known as Suras, as well as chapter and verse.

Footnote:

10 Matthew 2:12 NIV
11 al-Baqarah 2:4 Qu'ran

Bibliography:

Not needed unless citation is not from main text.

Pamphlet or Brochure with no indicated Author

Pamphlets and brochures are treated as books if you have the author information provided, as a corporate source if only that is given, and as a book without an author if you have neither. In that case, it is just listed by title, adding in whatever information you have regarding its publication date and location.

Footnote:

1 *Applying for Anonymity Status* (Vancouver, 2012).

Bibliography:

Applying for Anonymity Status. Vancouver, 2012.

Dissertation or Thesis

PhD Dissertations or Master's Thesis are listed as an article or story. List author first, use quotation marks for the title, and add either "PhD diss." or "Master's thesis" as needed. The dissertation or thesis may be published or unpublished. If it is published, used the city and publisher format as normal. If it is unpublished, just list the university and the year it was submitted (*see both examples below*):

Footnote (unpublished):

[12] Jane Doe, "Creating Auras of Invisibility" (PhD diss., University of Chicago, 2012), 8-9.

Footnote (published):

[13] Frank Smith, "Seeing those who won't be seen" (Master's thesis., Boston: University of Boston Press, 2013), 12-22.

Bibliography (unpublished):

Doe, Jane. "Creating Auras of Invisibility." PhD diss., University of Chicago, 2012.

Bibliography (published):

Smith, Frank. "Seeing those who won't be seen." Master's thesis., Boston: University of Boston Press, 2013.

Magazine Article / Newspaper Article

Magazine and newspaper sources are cited the same as articles and journals. Be aware of page numbering differences. If you access the article online, provide the link and access date (access date may be optional, depending on teacher's preferences).

Footnote from regular newspaper:

²² Janet Smyth, "Never Enough about Me," *Globe and Mail*, January 25, 2010, C12.

Footnote from online newspaper:

²² Janet Smyth, "Never Enough about Me," *Globe and Mail*, January 25, 2010, accessed February 28, 2010, www.globemail.com/34541.html.

Bibliography (both examples):

Smyth, Janet "Never Enough about Me." *Globe and Mail*, January 25, 2010.

Smyth, Janet. "Never Enough about Me." *Globe and Mail*, January 25, 2010. accessed February 28, 2010, www.globemail.com/34541.html.

Editorial or Letter to the Editor

Cite these exactly the same as the example above. If there is no title given for a letter to the editor, title it "Letter to the editor." Editorials will normally have a title, but in the rare instance that it does not, use "Editorial" in its place.

Article without an Author

Cite an article without an author by using the title of the article in place of the author's name. The rest follows normally. Use the indicator "in" to indicate it is part of a larger body of work. List the editor "ed." or compiler "comp." normally.

Footnote:

11 "Invisible Spouses," in *Anonymous Actions*, ed. John Doe et al. (Chicago: Chicago Press, 2011), 172.

Bibliography:

"Invisible Spouses," in *Anonymous Actions*, ed. John
Doe et al. Chicago: Chicago Press, 2011.

Article in a Scholarly Journal

Journals may have odd page numbering, or use volume and issue numbers. Provide what information is provided, or use the publication month and year for reference. Your bibliographical entry should list the page range of the complete article, even if you only cited from a small section. The example below has the volume number (104), the year (2009), and the page cited (44).

Footnote:

11 Joe Smith, "The Faceless Lost," *Classical Philosophy* 104 (2009): 44.

Bibliography:

Smith, Joe. "The Faceless Lost." *Classical Philosophy*
104 (2009): 38-49.

Website

It is necessary to list your date of access because web pages are often updated, and information available on one date may no longer be available later. Be sure to include the complete address for the site. Use *n.p.* if no publisher name is available and *n.d.* if no publishing date is given... and often it isn't. If there is no page author stated, then list from the topic or page title given.

Footnote (examples with and without an author):

[12] John Smith, "Joys of Beheading," *ChopChop.com*. n.d. (Feb 11, 2014).

[13] "Decapitation," *Wikipedia.org*. Jan 2013. (Feb 26, 2014).

[14] Slo Mo Guys, "Droplet collisions at 1600fps," *YouTube.com*. Feb 18, 2011. (Feb 26, 2014).

Bibliography:

Smith, John. "Joys of Beheading," *ChopChop.com*. (Feb 11, 2014). www.chopchop.com/beheading.html.

"Decapitation," *Wikipedia.org,* Jan 2013. (Feb 26, 2014). www.wikipedia.org/wiki/decapitation.

Slo Mo Guys. "Droplet collisions at 1600fps," *YouTube.com*. Feb 18, 2011. (Feb 26, 2014). http://www.youtube.com/watch?v=cNI-LIVs-to.

Online-Only Journal / Printed and Online Journal

Items found in online-only journals will not have page numbers, and so none are required. You do, however, need to provide the link to the source. For those that appear both online and in print, there should be a page number available.

Many only journals will provide a shortened link directly to the article, known as a DOI (Digital Object Identifier). These are important, because many links are generated dynamically based on search strings, and may not be permanent links. If this is not provided, then use the link given in the address bar.

The accessed date is also used, similar to a web site citation.

Footnote:

[1] John Smith and Jane Doe, "Origins of Anonymity in America," *American Journal of Sociology* 115 (2009): 411, (Feb 28, 2010), www.Journals.edu/123412.

Bibliography:

Smith, John and Jane Doe, "Origins of Anonymity in America," *American Journal of Sociology* 115 (2009): 411. (Feb 28, 2010). www.Journals.edu/123412.

Online Database

The format here is exactly the same as the one above, but add in the database service used (in the example below, *EBSCO*).

Footnote:

[1] John Smith and Jane Doe, "Origins of Anonymity in America," *American Journal of Sociology* 115 (2009): 411, (Feb 28, 2010), EBSCO, www.ebscohost.com/123412

Bibliography:

Smith, John and Jane Doe, "Origins of Anonymity in America," *American Journal of Sociology* 115 (2009): 411. (Feb 28, 2010). EBSCO. www.ebscohost.com/123412

E-mail message content

E-mail and text messages may be cited in running text ("In a text message to the author on March 1, 2010, John Doe stated . . .") instead of in a footnote, and they are rarely listed in a bibliography. The following example shows the more formal version of a note.

Footnote:

[1] John Doe, e-mail message to author, February 28, 2010.

Bibliography:

Not needed.

Listserv / Blog / Reddit / Tweet / Facebook Sources

Blog entries or comments may be cited in running text ("In a comment posted to *The Anonymize Blog* on February 13, 2012, . . .") instead of in a note, and they are commonly omitted from a bibliography. The following examples show the more formal versions of the citations.

There is no need to add *pseud.* after an apparently fictitious or informal name. (If an access date is required, add it before the URL).

For Facebook posts or status updates, that identifier can be added after the date and time of posting (see second footnote example). Facebook posts are generally not listed in the bibliography section.

Footnote:

[1] JackBean76, February 13, 2012 (7:03 p.m.), comment on SlayerBoi, "Can I vanish?," *Anonymizer Blog*, February 21, 2012, http://anonymizer.blogspot.com/123354.html.

[11] Joe Smith, March 11, 2013 (12:10 a.m.), status update, March 12, 2013, http://facebook.com/joe.smith.

Bibliography:

Anonymizer Blog. http://anonymizer.blogspot.com.

Film source in Theatre / Out on DVD or Blu-ray

If citing a film or performance still in theatre or on stage, list the name of the film or production, the director, and the year it was released. If the source is out of DVD or Blu-ray, include the publisher or distributor and the date it was released.

If the item is an episode in a longer series, place the episode title in quotation marks, and the series name in italics.

Footnote (Movie in Theatre):

[12] *Dial M for Murder*, directed by Alfred Hitchcock (1954).

Footnote (Movie on DVD):

[12] *Dial M for Murder*, directed by Alfred Hitchcock (California: Warner Home Video, 2004), DVD.

Bibliography (Movie in Theatre):

Dial M for Murder. Directed by Alfred Hitchcock. 1954.

Bibliography (Movie on DVD):

Dial M for Murder. Directed by Alfred Hitchcock. California: Warner Home Video, 2004. DVD.

Radio and Television Programs

Radio and Television programs are listed with the name of the program in quotation marks, and the name of the show in italics. Radio stations are listed according to their call letters, full name, and date of institution. Television stations are listed according to their identifier and first air date only (placed in brackets). The "Author" of the piece is normally the director or producer. If the first air date or date of institution is unavailable, it may be omitted.

Footnote (Television):

[32] Richard Stomps, "The Last Gig on Earth," *Love is in the Air*, aired March 12, 2011 (Sydney: ABC TV, 2006), Television broadcast.

Footnote (Radio):

[32] Joe Smith, "Fading Forever," *Morning Talk Radio*, aired March 2, 2001 (Vancouver: CKNW Talk Radio, 1986), Radio broadcast.

Bibliography (Television):

Stomps, Richard. "The Last Gig on Earth." *Love is in the Air*. Aired March 12, 2011. Sydney: ABC TV, 2006. Television broadcast.

Bibliography (Radio):

Smith, Joe. "Fading Forever," *Morning Talk Radio*, aired March 2, 2001. Vancouver: CKNW Talk Radio, 1986. Radio broadcast.

Music and Sound Recordings

Music and sound recordings are listed similarly to citations from DVD or Blu-ray sources. If you are citing a single track from an album, list that title in quotation marks, and the album source in italics. The production company, year of release, and medium used are listed following that.

Footnote (Full Album):

[10] Pink Floyd, *Delicate Sound of Thunder*, CBS Columbia, 1988, Compact disc.

Footnote (Single Song):

[10] Pink Floyd, "Sorrow," *Delicate Sound of Thunder*, CBS Columbia, 1988, MP3.

Bibliography (Full Album):

Pink Floyd. *Delicate Sound of Thunder*. CBS Columbia, 1988. Compact disc.

Bibliography (Single Song):

Pink Floyd. "Sorrow," *Delicate Sound of Thunder*. CBS Columbia, 1988. MP3.

PERSONAL NOTES

30070251R00085